WHOLE FOOD ENERGY

200 ALL-NATURAL RECIPES TO PREPARE, REFUEL AND RECOVER

First published in the UK in 2016 by
APPLE PRESS
74–77 White Lion Street
London N1 9PF
United Kingdom

www.apple-press.com

This book was conceived, designed and produced by
Quantum Books Ltd
6 Blundell Street
London N7 9BH
United Kingdom

Publisher: Kerry Enzor
Editorial: Philippa Davis and Emma Harverson
Copyeditor: Abi Waters
Nutritional Evaluator: Anne Marie Berggren
Designer: Rupert Gowar-Cliffe
Cover Design: Tokiko Morishima
Photographer: Simon Pask
Production Manager: Zarni Win

ISBN: 978-1-8454-3634-6

Printed in China by 1010 Printing International Ltd.

2 4 6 8 10 9 7 5 3 1

QUMWFE3

Author photograph: © 2015 ImageLinkPhoto.com
/ Geoff Chesman

Disclaimer
The medical and/or nutritional information in this book is not intended to be a substitute
for professional medical advice, diagnosis or treatment. There is the possibility of
allergic or other adverse reactions from the use of any ingredients mentioned in this
book. In particular, those with medical conditions or allergies, infants, the elderly
and pregnant women should seek the advice of their doctor or other qualified health
provider with any questions they may have. Never disregard professional medical
advice or delay seeking it because of something you have read in this book. Readers
should be aware that knowledge of nutrition and medicine is constantly evolving. The
authors, editors and publisher exclude all liability to the extent permitted by law for any
errors or omissions in this book and for any loss damage or expense (whether direct or
indirect) suffered by a third party relying on any information contained in this book.

WHOLE FOOD
ENERGY

**200 ALL-NATURAL RECIPES TO
PREPARE, REFUEL AND RECOVER**

ELISE MUSELES

APPLE

CONTENTS

INTRODUCTION

I would love to invite you over for tea and an afternoon pick-me-up. We could sip on my signature turmeric latte and have an array of healthy snacks to choose from that pack in nutrition from whole food ingredients.

You'll find my kitchen filled with homemade energy bars and balls, jars of DIY nut milk and fresh, colourful fruits and vegetables to turn into smoothies and nutrient-dense juices.

But my kitchen wasn't always so well stocked. In fact, it was quite the opposite. Snacks and in-between-meal nutrients were an afterthought. Packaged protein bars were my mainstay source of nutrition … sometimes even substituting for meals themselves.

Now I look back and think about all those times when I got distracted by my grumbling stomach in the middle of spin class, or wanted to go into child's pose (and rest!) halfway through my yoga session instead of flowing on my mat. All those times when I came home from work, both irritable and impatient at 5 P.M. and snapped at my kids or husband, or stood in front of the larder taking bites of everything in sight, then was too full and upset with myself to eat dinner. All the times when I tried to concentrate in an important client meeting but found myself unable to focus, and the times when I packed up a coolbag of ready-to-go snacks for my kids to keep them properly nourished on long days … and packed nothing for myself.

Of course, now I understand that what I really needed to save myself from experiencing plummeting blood sugar and low energy was actually so simple: I needed to reframe the way I thought about feeding my body and think beyond three square meals a day. I needed to find ways to nourish myself in-between meals and during those times when I couldn't sit down to a typical breakfast, lunch or dinner. I needed to prioritize my health by feeding my body whole, real foods all day long.

I hear the same story from so many of my friends and clients that they're ridiculously busy; they're convinced they don't have time to do everything they want to do *and* take care of themselves. But one of the most important lessons I've learned is that 'busy' is not an excuse. It's all the more reason to focus on nourishing your body.

So, I developed recipes that you can prepare in bulk and grab from the fridge on the way out the door. I made fruit and nut bars that you can nibble between meals and smoothies to drink during the morning madness. With a little planning and forethought, we can all eat the nutritious, energizing whole foods our bodies crave without derailing our busy schedules.

Every recipe in this book is packed with nutrients and health benefits. They're also delicious and free from all the additives of ready-made products. In the old days, healthy food was considered bland and boring. This book is anything but. There are anti-inflammatory spices and herbs mixed with fresh ingredients to give you the energy and health benefits in the tastiest way possible, so that you can keep up with the demands of your active life – whether that's running after your kids, balancing work and the gym or simply hopping on your bike and enjoying some fresh air on the weekend.

Whole foods and the energy that comes from eating this way can change your entire life. It can be the difference between breezing through an afternoon with mental clarity and enthusiasm versus wanting to have a nap on your desk as your eyes start to drift away from the computer screen. It can be the difference between finishing your morning run exhilarated versus crawling with pained muscles for that last mile. It can be the difference between keeping up with your life versus having the enthusiasm and stamina to live your life.

Whether you're already whipping up smoothies and juicing your greens or whether you're completely new to the concept of eating whole foods, there is something for everyone.

I can't wait for you to dig in and start shifting your approach to how you nourish your body on the go and in-between meals! When you start blending, puréeing, baking and assembling these easy-to-make recipes, you can invite me into your kitchen for tea and healthy homemade snacks. I'll be right over.

Here's to whole food energy!

LET'S GET STARTED

The recipes in this book have been carefully designed with the busy, active person in mind; each is quick and easy to prepare and perfectly balanced to meet your energy needs. This book is packed with information to make it easy for you to identify the recipes to match your specific energy needs; use the tags and colour-coding (see keys on page 9) to quickly guide you.

How to find the recipe you need
The recipes are divided into chapters by food type so that you can quickly search for the perfect smoothie, morning bite or dessert. You can also use the indexes at the back of the book to find recipes by key nutrient or nutritional tag.

Tags to highlight benefits
Each recipe section is tagged for key nutritional benefits (see key opposite), so you can choose the recipe to meet your needs.

Make your own staples
Find recipes for all your whole food staples on pages 157–165. Lots of recipes in the book use plant-based milks and butters. Instead of ready-made varieties of these household staples, learn how to make your own delicious dairy-free butters, milks, cream and yogurts.

Nutritionally balanced content
At the back of the book, pages 166–173, you can find additional nutritional information, including the recommended daily values for key nutrients. There are also comprehensive indexes for each of the whole food tags (see key opposite), along with the top five recipes for vital nutrients to support a healthy lifestyle, such as protein, potassium and vitamins A and C.

About each recipe group
Before you start, find out the yield and serving size for each recipe, plus the preparation and cooking times and storage information.

Nutritional information
A breakdown of key nutritional information is provided for each recipe.

Using the colour-coding
Each of the recipes has been colour-coded so that you can quickly determine if a recipe is energizing for when you need a kick-start, sustaining to keep you going or replenishing to wind down and restore. (For more information on energizing, sustaining and replenishing, see pages 14–15.)

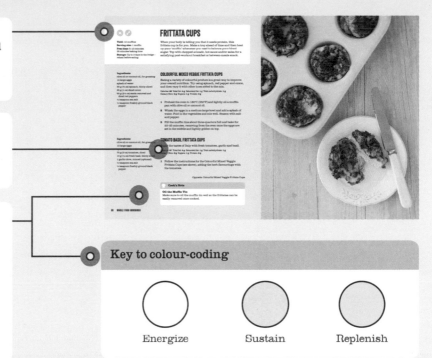

Key to colour-coding

Energize   Sustain   Replenish

HOW TO USE THE WHOLE FOOD ENERGY TAGS

Throughout the book recipes are tagged with specific nutritional values to help you identify the best recipe to support your energy needs. Simply flip through the pages to find foods that will provide fast-release energy, give you an extra dose of calcium or help your muscles recover after a workout.

 Muscle repairing: A good source of protein for supporting muscle repair after exercise.

Anti-inflammatory: This book is filled with anti-inflammatory recipes. The true anti-inflammatory superstars, containing omega-3 fatty acids and/or a dose of healing spices, are flagged here.

 Slow-release energy: Well balanced to prevent blood sugar spikes and provide energy that lasts.

 Healthy bones: Rich in calcium, magnesium and vitamins C and D – all essential for bone health.

 Portable: Designed as grab-and-go options, to be taken with you on a busy day.

 Fast-release energy: With a higher ratio of carbs to fat and protein these recipes provide fuel for activities that require a lot of energy. Fast-release recipes don't have a lot of fibre, fat or protein, as these all slow the absorption of carbohydrates.

 Mood enhancing: Include whole foods that boost serotonin levels, such as cacao, watermelon and tomatoes.

PART ONE: INTRODUCING WHOLE FOODS

WHOLE FOOD 101

Before we dive in, it is important to understand exactly what whole foods are and why they are so valuable for supporting an active lifestyle. This chapter introduces you to some of the incredible benefits you can enjoy when you eat a diet filled with these nutrient-dense foods. Read on!

WHAT ARE WHOLE FOODS?

Of course you know that roasted veggie crisps you slice and bake yourself are a whole food, while those powder-coated cheese-flavoured crisps aren't. But even the most savvy among us can get confused when we step into one of those high-end natural grocery stores. Is that macaroni and cheese claiming to be 100-per cent natural a whole food? What about the organic soup in a carton? Or the dairy-free coconut ice cream? There's a whole food grey zone that can confuse the best of us. Simply put, whole foods are foods that have not been processed or refined and are as close to their natural state as possible. They're free from additives and artificial substances.

WHOLE FOOD SHOPPING TIPS

1 Buy food that's as close to its original form as possible.

2 Buy food with as little packaging as possible.

3 If you do buy something in a package, choose food with the shortest list of ingredients and with the least amount of processing.

WHY ARE WHOLE FOODS GOOD FOR YOU?

While whole foods are delicious, there are tons of other benefits as well. For one thing, they're rich in phytochemicals (beneficial compounds produced by plants, including antioxidants, flavonoids, phytonutrients and more). Mounting evidence shows these powerful nutrients can help prevent heart disease, diabetes, high blood pressure and even cancer. Whole foods contain more vitamins and nutrients than their processed counterparts and have more fibre and good fats.

Your body will instantly recognize that you are flooding it with nutrients when you eat whole foods. Whole foods are also more likely to level out your blood sugar so that you're more patient and inspired. They help you power through your workouts and meetings. In short, whole foods give you the energy you need for your busy life.

When you cook with whole foods and make your own meals and snacks, you know exactly what's going into each dish. You don't have to worry about your peanut allergy or your spouse's gluten issues. You'll never bite into an energy bar that you made and be surprised by ingredients tucked inside.

HOW DOES THIS BOOK HELP?

Now that we understand the importance of feeding our bodies and minds real whole foods with all the nutrients intact, you might be wondering why the focus of this book is on snacks and smaller bites. Why not main dishes and full meals? Of course, it goes without saying that I'm an advocate of whole foods all day long. Sure, you might sit down to dinner on most nights and enjoy grilled salmon, baked sweet potato and broccoli; or perhaps you're religious about having porridge with blueberries and walnuts all winter long. But in today's world, where busy is the new normal, we don't always have time to eat a leisurely meal. Plus, when we do put in such long days, our bodies need to be fuelled in-between those meals.

The tendency is to overlook what to eat in those situations, and more often than not, it's a time when many of us fall short on nutrition. We grab whatever we can in our hurried state. It's usually about convenience, which typically means packaged and processed food. This book will redefine our vision of 'convenience food'. The new convenience is all about prepping, planning and stocking the fridge/freezer/larder in advance, so that you can have home-cooked, portable, grab-and-go snacks and small bites available. When these new kinds of 'convenience foods' are made in your very own kitchen using whole food ingredients, they can help to improve overall health, curb cravings, fight weight gain, regulate mood, boost brain power and give you the energy you need to keep going all day. How convenient is that?!

ENERGIZE, SUSTAIN, REPLENISH

Throughout the book, you will notice the pages are colour-coded to categorize recipes into groups: Energize, Sustain or Replenish. While there is some overlap, these categories are meant to help you choose which recipes support you best throughout your day. Use these suggestions as guidelines, and always adjust your choices depending on how you feel.

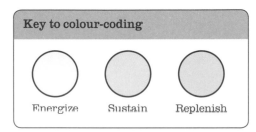

Key to colour-coding

Energize   Sustain   Replenish

ENERGIZE

TO KICK-START YOUR SYSTEM

When it's 6 A.M. on an overcast Monday morning, you want something more inspiring than a bowl of cold cereal. You'll also need energy that will last longer than what you get from a cup of coffee.

The recipes colour-coded for 'energize' are foods that will give you a boost anytime you need it. These recipes will ramp up your energy with an adequate supply of complex carbohydrates, your body's preferred fuel. You'll find many of these recipes filled with natural sugar from fruits or natural sweeteners such as honey and maple syrup. Because this category is meant to give you the burst you need before a workout or to jump-start your day, there are recipes that offer a combination of both slow- and fast-release energy. Porridges and overnight oats sweetened naturally with fruit, nutrient-dense smoothies made with bananas and energy bars and balls make up the bulk of these recipes. You will also find foods in 'energize' that are easy on the stomach so you can eat them prior to an active workout and not worry about digestive distress.

As long as you can listen to your body and determine how and when to load up on these foods, the 'energize' recipes will help you wake up – and stay that way!

SUSTAIN

TO KEEP YOU GOING

If you're looking at your calendar and you know that today is going to be an endurance race, rather than a sprint, you'll want to pull a few ideas from the 'sustain' recipes.

The recipes in 'sustain' are loaded with complex carbohydrates and also contain adequate protein for slow-burning energy and just the right amount of healthy fat to keep you satisfied for the distance. Think thick-and-creamy smoothies, nut butter-coated granola and muffins flavoured with anti-inflammatory spices. There are also lots of portable options such as trail mixes, fruit-and-nut energy bars, spiced nuts and roasted chickpeas – perfect to tuck into your bag, stash in your desk drawer or take with you on a longer run, walk or bike ride. These foods will help you stay centred and sane, even if it has been many hours since your last full meal.

REPLENISH

TO WIND DOWN AND RESTORE

Healthy food can be filled with nutrients and be comforting at the same time. That's where the 'replenish' recipes come into play.

Most of us imagine piles of pasta or warm gooey chocolate chip cookies when we think of cosy foods. But there are so many whole foods that can nourish and make us feel good, both physically and psychologically. Imagine sipping on a warm Spiced Vanilla Almond Milk (see page 63) in front of a crackling fire, or finishing a hot yoga class and having a Mango Refresher Slushy (see page 45) to enjoy while you cool down. I created these recipes for those moments, not only to help you replenish your energy with specific nutrient-dense ingredients, but also for when you want to feed your body and soul. These recipes will flood your body with an extra dose of TLC any time of day when you need a boost.

HEALTH FOOD MYTH BUSTING

There is a bewildering amount of advice on health foods – some bad, some good. The best way to approach healthy eating is with an open mind. Pay attention to your individual needs rather than any 'food rules'. Test out different recipes and notice if you make any quick judgments. If you find yourself falling prey to nutritional myths, ask yourself where this comes from and decide whether it is time to change your thinking. To separate fact from fiction, let's look at some of the most common assumptions.

#1 MYTH: Fat is bad (or fat in my food means fat on my body).

BUSTED: Not all fat is created equal. The key is to avoid the saturated animal fats and trans fats, which can be detrimental to your health. Focus on the good-for-you fats that come from avocados, nuts, seeds, olive oil, coconut oil, coconut and fatty fish like salmon, as these fats are loaded with health benefits. Aside from keeping your blood sugar stable, the fat in these healthy foods can help you absorb all those powerful nutrients that you are getting from your other whole foods. Fat is also the beauty macronutrient that can make your hair, skin and nails look their best. Healthy fat can aid in controlling appetite, because you feel satisfied and full when you have a serving of it with your meal, and it can give you sustained energy since it takes longer to break down in your system. Let's also not forget that fat can add wonderful flavour to food, too. In short, good fat is your friend.

#2 MYTH: Carbs are not good, and I need to count them.

BUSTED: Carbohydrates have been vilified ever since high-protein diets gained popularity. Because carbohydrates are your body's primary energy source, it's important to feed your body the right kind of carbohydrates throughout the day. Like fats, not all carbohydrates are created equal. The carbohydrates coming from whole grains, pulses, fruits and vegetables will provide you with fibre, phytonutrients (including antioxidants) and sustained slow-release energy.

On the flip side, the carbohydrates that can zap your body of energy (and give all carbs a bad rap) are the refined grains and quick sources of sugar from the various sugars themselves, and products made with enriched flours and processed ingredients. Your body processes these foods quickly, which can wreak havoc on your blood sugar, leaving you feeling drained and fatigued. When you fill up on whole foods, you're feeding your body carbohydrates with all the nutrients intact that will give you energy to support your busy and active lifestyle.

Note: For a more detailed discussion on carbohydrates and whole foods, see Myth 9, page 18.

#3 MYTH: Healthy food is bland and boring.

BUSTED: Scroll through the photos in any health-focused magazine or Instagram feed and you'll see vibrant colours and the use of whole food ingredients in novel and creative ways. There are lots of opportunities to combine colours and textures and create healthy food that is tasty, innovative and interesting. In this book, you are going to think outside the traditional box with some healthy twists on classics – hello Baked Chewy Oat Chocolate Chip Cookies (see page 141) made without any refined sugars or white flour.

#4 MYTH: Cooking is time consuming.

BUSTED: Sure, if you are comparing the time it takes to prepare home-cooked meals to the time it takes to get a takeaway, then you're right. But within the parameters of cooking, there are varying degrees of time and effort required to put together a healthy meal or snack from scratch. This book was created with the busy person in mind, which means most of the recipes can be made quickly, and others can be prepped in batches so you can cook once and then eat that snack three or four times, or more!

#5 MYTH: Healthy food is expensive.

BUSTED: It's true that some healthy foods cost more money than their processed counterparts. But, there are ways to buy, save and eat whole foods on a budget. You just need to shop cleverly. A few ideas to keep the cost down include: eating what's in season, purchasing produce weekly at a local farmers' market, joining a CSA (community supported agriculture), buying in bulk, looking for sales and stocking up or freezing produce when it's in season (and less expensive) to use later.

#6 MYTH: Cravings should be conquered.

BUSTED: Our cravings serve as message carriers. It's our body's way of speaking to us to tell us what we need. Next time you have a craving, don't think of it as something bad and brush it off. Instead, become curious and ask yourself: Did I eat enough? Am I depleted of a specific nutrient or mineral? Are my meals properly balanced? Is this about the food? If you dig deep and listen, you'll usually find the answers.

#7 MYTH: I need to follow a healthy eating plan perfectly all the time.

BUSTED: A commitment to a healthy lifestyle and healthy eating isn't a commitment to a straight and narrow path. It's a journey. Know that there will be ups and downs and twists and turns. It's all part of it. When you give yourself permission to not be 'perfect' all the time, it keeps things real and makes getting back on track much easier to do. Just because you eat a slice of cake to celebrate a birthday doesn't mean the day is a write-off and you should eat lots more processed foods for the rest of the day. Practise progress over perfection.

#8 MYTH: I'm too busy to start a new healthy eating plan.

BUSTED: If your life is full and busy, then you could wait for a very long time for things to slow down. Any shift in habits that is meant to be long-term and sustainable needs to work with your lifestyle. That means you can start integrating some of the concepts into your routine right now, no matter how busy you are at the moment. Keep it simple and add in one new recipe a week while you adjust. Perhaps the Blueberry Cashew Overnight Oats (see page 71) are the perfect start to your jam-packed day. The changes don't need to happen all at once. Every step counts.

#9 MYTH: I won't get enough carbs or protein from whole foods.

BUSTED: You can supply your body with adequate amounts of all the macronutrients (carbohydrates, protein and fat) with whole foods alone. Carbohydrates are a vital source of energy for your body, while proteins support healthy growth and maintenance. When you eat nutrient-dense whole foods, your body is more able to digest and assimilate all the nutrients. By choosing whole foods over processed foods, you're giving your body the highest fuel it can use to function properly – whether that's repairing itself after a heavy lifting session or sleeping more soundly.

#10

MYTH: Snacking in-between meals is a bad habit.

BUSTED: When you go six or seven hours between lunch and dinner and have meetings, errands and a workout in-between, it would be doing your body a disservice not to snack. Eating whole food snacks to get you from one meal to the next will actually work for you, not against you. It will help regulate your blood sugar and energy levels. You will avoid the 4 P.M. slump – or even the late-night mindless eating – when you have planned healthy bites accessible. You're also more likely to make sound choices at your next meal if you don't arrive at the table starving!

GET EQUIPPED

It's so much more fun to cook with the right tools. Nobody wants to chop carrots or heads of leafy greens with a blunt knife! To get you started, here's a checklist of my favourite kitchen tools. While you don't need to purchase all these items overnight, you can do so over the years as you expand your collection of gadgets.

Glass Storage Containers

Several studies have found that most plastics release a hormone similar to oestrogen. Use glass storage containers to sidestep that altogether.

Chef's Knife

A good, regularly sharpened knife makes cooking faster and more enjoyable, and it's safer because the blade won't stick.

High-Speed Liquidizer

This is more of an investment piece because liquidizers can be really expensive, but I use my high-speed liquidizer every single day for smoothies, dressings, nut milks, desserts, soups and more. If you have a normal liquidizer or food processor, don't worry; it will work for this book, but it might just take a little longer to blend to a smooth consistency.

Food Processor

Food processors can work wonders with whole foods. Many of the dips and energy ball and truffle recipes call for a food processor. This is a piece of equipment that you will use over and over.

Juicer

Juicers separate the juice from the insoluble fibre in fruits, vegetables and herbs. Drinking fresh juice floods your body with highly absorbable nutrients and enzymes to help boost your health and energy levels.

Nut Milk Bags

Homemade nut milk is cheaper, healthier and usually more delicious than the ready-made versions (see page 162).

Microplane Grater

This is basically a very sharp shredder. Once you start using freshly ground ginger and turmeric, you'll never go back. Many of the recipes call for zest, and the microplane is an easy way to quickly add zest to your recipes.

Lemon Squeezer

Two-armed lemon squeezers work so much better than old-fashioned citrus juicers.

Muffin Tins

You can't make muffins without the tins, and I prefer the ones that do not have the non-stick coating to limit the amount of chemical exposure from the tins.

Baking Paper

Baking paper has multiple practical uses: It can be used to line trays for easy cleaning, and it can be used to store energy bars, chocolate barks, energy balls and muffins so that the food doesn't stick together. It also comes in handy to place on the worktop when measuring cacao powder and turmeric to prevent any unwanted stains.

Wide-Mouth Mason Jars

Wide-mouth mason jars are easy to clean; easy to fill; and perfectly portioned for smoothies, juices, overnight oats, trail mixes, granolas, parfaits and just about everything.

Small Ice Cream Scoop

These scoops are a great way to measure out portions without getting your hands messy. It's the perfect size for the raw cookies and some of the delicious energy balls and bites in this book.

STOCK UP

If the right tools make cooking more fun, a well-stocked larder makes cooking about a million times easier. Of course, many of these recipes call for fresh fruit and vegetables – and you can't really stockpile fresh raspberries. You can, however, make sure that you've got all the other ingredients ready to go when you decide to whip up a batch of Spiced Roasted Carrot Hummus (see page 98) or Almond Butter and Chocolate Banana Ice Cream (see page 147).

You don't need to buy all of the ingredients listed below at once – slowly add them to your kitchen repertoire over time. You'll probably notice that there are certain nuts, seeds and spices that you use over and over, so make sure you have these on hand.

RAW NUTS AND SEEDS

Use these to make your DIY nut milks, top smoothies, add to trail mixes, mix into granolas and tuck into energy bars and balls. I like to buy all my nuts raw, then roast or toast as needed.

- Cashews
- Almonds
- Brazil nuts
- Hazelnuts
- Walnuts
- Pecans
- Macadamia nuts
- Pistachios
- Pumpkin seeds
- Sunflower seeds (shelled)
- Flax seeds and flax meal – flax meal is ground flax seeds, which make the flax more digestible. You can buy flax meal from health food stores or grind your own flax seeds.

BEANS AND PULSES

Beans and pulses are an amazing, cheap source of protein, and they last forever! If you're feeling ambitious, buy them in dried form and

soak them overnight before cooking, or buy organic tinned versions. Keep them on hand for savoury dips and Roasted Chickpeas (see page 108).

- Haricot beans
- Chickpeas
- Black beans

WHOLE GRAINS AND WHOLE GRAIN FLOURS

Don't let that low-carb nonsense scare you! The complex carbohydrates we get from whole grains help us sustain slow-burning energy over long days and supply us with fibre to keep us full.

- Rolled and/or steel-cut oats (gluten-free if necessary)
- Oat flour – or you can make you own by grinding oats in a food processor or liquidizer.
- Quinoa
- Buckwheat
- Brown rice flour
- Almond flour – or make your own by grinding 110–200 g (4–7 oz) of blanched almonds in a high-speed liquidizer. Blend for 10 seconds or until you have a fine powder.
- Chickpea flour
- Coconut flour
- Quinoa flour
- Millet flour

NUT AND SEED BUTTERS

While there are some fun DIY nut butters in this book, sometimes it's handy to have a ready-made jar on hand. There is a variety of nut and seed butters available from health food stores, just make sure to buy organic, unsweetened, unsalted and non-GMO when possible.

- Coconut butter – different from coconut oil, this is a great option to toss into smoothies for a nut-free version.
- Tahini (sesame seed paste)

DRIED FRUIT

Dried fruit is portable, healthy and has a long shelf life. It's in many of the recipes, including trail mixes (see page 88), energy bars (see page 113), granolas (see page 84) and chocolate barks (see page 154). When possible, buy unsweetened dried fruit that's labelled as 'unsulphured'. Unsulphured dried fruit won't look as brightly coloured, but it's preservative-free and tastes so much better!

- Golden raisins
- Goji berries
- Shredded coconut and coconut flakes
- Dates – I like Medjool.
- Figs
- Apricots
- Cherries
- Cranberries
- Pineapple
- Blueberries
- Strawberries
- Apples
- Mangoes
- Mulberries

BAKING EXTRAS

Have these basic baking ingredients on hand for muffins, chocolate bark and crackers.

- Baking powder (aluminium-free)
- Bicarbonate of soda
- Tapioca starch or arrowroot
- Pumpkin purée – cartons are best, but if not available, buy organic tinned.
- Tinned coconut milk
- Cacao nibs

- Raw cacao powder – this is not only high in antioxidants but also a purer form of cocoa powder. You can use cocoa powder as a substitute if cacao is not available.

FLAVOUR BOOSTERS

There are lots of delicious, healthy condiments and flavourings you can use that up the taste and the nutritional content of your food. Vinegars help stabilize blood sugar, and mustard has been shown to improve immunity.

- Balsamic vinegar
- Red wine vinegar
- Apple cider vinegar
- Mustard
- Nutritional yeast – this is an inactivate yeast that adds a cheesy flavour to the Cashew Cream Cheese, Roasted Chickpeas and Spiced Nuts (see pages 102, 108 and 110). It can also be added to dressings and sauces.
- Vegetable broth
- Pure vanilla extract
- Pure mint extract
- Pure almond extract
- Vanilla beans
- Tamari (gluten-free soy sauce)

FROZEN FRUIT

When fresh fruit is too expensive or out of season, frozen makes for a great stand-in – the fruit you buy in the freezer section is frozen during peak season. Plus, smoothies get their thick consistency with frozen fruit. If possible, buy organic. Also, you can freeze your own if you buy too many bananas.

- Berries (strawberries, raspberries, blueberries, blackberries)
- Bananas – peel and then slice them before they get too brown. Store in the freezer to make smoothies and banana ice cream.

- Pineapple
- Mango
- Peaches
- Pears – cut and core ripe pears to freeze. They can be used in porridge or to add amazing creaminess to smoothies.
- Cherries
- Avocado – buy a bunch of avocados at the height of the season, and when they're perfectly ripe, cut them in half, peel them and freeze.
- Greens – keep frozen spinach, kale and/or Swiss chard to have on hand to toss into smoothies.

NATURAL SWEETENERS

These natural sweeteners are still sugars, so they should be used in moderation, but they do have the added bonus of having some healthy nutrients.

- Pure maple syrup
- Raw honey
- Medjool dates
- Apple sauce – particularly useful for baked goods.

HERBS AND SPICES

Herbs do not just add flavour to recipes, they also come with health benefits. Cinnamon helps control blood sugar, while ginger aids digestion and is an anti-inflammatory. Garlic protects against heart disease, and turmeric regulates hormones, protects against cancer and is an anti-inflammatory. Because it's so easy to include herbs and spices in recipes, it's important to keep a well-stocked larder.

- Cinnamon
- Cardamom
- Cumin
- Ginger
- Nutmeg
- Turmeric
- Garlic granules
- Onion powder
- Cayenne pepper
- Paprika
- Chilli flakes
- Basil
- Oregano
- Cloves
- Sea salt – while it tastes similar to table salt, sea salt is richer in minerals and a little lower in sodium.
- Chilli powder
- Wasabi powder
- Black pepper
- Curry powder

OILS

Oils add much-needed healthy fats to your diet. Gram for gram, fats are the most efficient source of food energy. They help you build healthy cells, improve your brain function and regulate your hormones. They help your body absorb vitamins and form a protective cushion for your organs. Just as importantly, they're delicious and look gorgeous drizzled atop a slice of avocado or a bowl of freshly made hummus.

- Extra virgin olive oil
- Toasted sesame oil – a little goes a long way!
- Coconut oil – heart-healthy, with antifungal and antibacterial properties and a high smoking point.
- Avocado oil
- Walnut oil
- Grapeseed oil – a neutral cooking oil that can be used in granolas and muffins in place of olive or coconut oil, which have a stronger flavour.

NUT AND SEED MILKS

You'll find recipes for DIY plant-based milks on pages 162–165, but it's also nice to keep a few cartons of unsweetened nut milks on hand for spontaneous smoothies.

Non-dairy milk is an alternative for people who are lactose-intolerant; it's a good choice for all of us because it's less likely to include pesticides, hormones or antibiotics. Most non-dairy products also happen to be better for the environment because the production process consumes fewer resources.

- Almond milk
- Hemp milk
- Cashew milk
- Coconut milk

SAMPLE WHOLE FOOD DAY PLANS

Wondering how to find the right recipe to suit your energy needs? Here are a few sample daily plans showing you how to choose the best whole food snacks and light bites throughout the day.

FOR THE PARENT JUGGLING SCHOOL RUNS AND PLAYDATES

FOR THE BUSY DAYS

FOR THE MIDWEEK WORKOUTS

FOR THE WEEKEND ADVENTURERS

FOR THE DAYS WHEN YOU NEED SOME EXTRA TLC

SET YOURSELF UP FOR WHOLE FOOD SUCCESS

Packing your diet full of whole foods will help you feel naturally energized and give your body all the nutrients it needs to perform at its best. Before you race ahead to try some of the delicious recipes in this book, take a moment to set yourself up for healthy eating success with these simple tips.

CREATE THE RIGHT MIND-SET

I spent years of my life over-complicating health. I would track every carb and calorie and berate myself when I ate 'bad' food.

Imagine my surprise when I realized that healthy food could be easy. And fun! I discovered that I could spend one afternoon prepping most of what I would eat for the rest of the week – and when I ate that colourful, whole food, I would feel satisfied and nourished.

In the recipes that follow, you will find calories, carbs and nutrition profiles, but I would like you to use them as guides or simply view them as neutral pieces of information. I encourage you to check in with your body as you experiment with these new recipes. Rather than depending on a list of carb, fat and protein counts to tell you what to eat, consider how your body *feels* when you eat a Coconut, Almond and Chocolate Power Bar (see page 119) before your spinning class. Don't let a list of numbers run the show.

EAT MINDFULLY

When you hear 'mindful eating', do you imagine yourself sipping a cup of green tea in a quiet restaurant while a gong rings in the distance?

Thankfully, eating mindfully doesn't require Zen-like patience or a tea master. Of course, a lot of us are eating in the car or at our desk in-between meetings. It might not be possible to turn every meal or snack into a deeply calming, centring experience. However, it is possible to give your undivided attention to your food when you're eating it, even if that is just for a few minutes.

Instead of eating your Lemon Drop Energy Balls (see page 126) in the front seat of the car, what if you got up, walked to a bench, and ate them there? What if you took the time to put your Tomato Basil Frittata Cup (see page 80) on an actual plate once you arrived at your desk? And then swivelled your desk chair towards the window instead of your computer screen?

What if you made a commitment to just eat while you're eating? When you sit down, fully engage your senses and connect with your food, you'll not only feel more satisfied, you'll also notice what nourishes you … and what doesn't.

STRESS LESS

If you are always on the go and have lots of commitments and interests, it goes without saying that you will sometimes feel overwhelmed and as if there aren't enough hours in the day to keep up.

The stress that can come from being overcommitted and being stretched too thin can impact your health and overall well-being. Our bodies respond to stress by releasing cortisol (the stress hormone), which can have negative effects on metabolism, digestion, nutrient assimilation and more. While stress is inevitable and there are some stressors that you can't control, you can control how you respond to the stress.

When you feed your body with the right nutrients – whole foods – you're better equipped to handle whatever comes your way. By eating foods that help you maintain even blood sugar levels, you will then feel calm and stable. You're less likely to get bent out of shape when the stressful situations arise. In other words, nourishing your body with whole food energy can be an integral part of your stress management.

MAKE IT YOUR OWN

While I have poured tons of work and love and energy into these recipes, they're not written in stone.

If an ingredient doesn't appeal to you, swap it for another. If you don't have a certain spice on hand, try something else! If you have an allergy or sensitivity, check the variation.

View these recipes as a framework to build on. They are meant to inspire you to put your own personal stamp on them. So go ahead: experiment, alter, substitute and nourish your mind and body with delicious whole foods.

PART TWO: THE RECIPES

Note: Yields and nutritional information will vary depending on product size and equipment used. Recipes throughout use medium-sized produce unless otherwise noted. Nutritional information provided is per serving.

SMOOTHIES

Smoothies are the busy person's solution to loading up on whole foods. In minutes, you can whip up a tasty and nutrient-dense creation tailored to your specific nutritional needs. From energizing smoothies in a rainbow of colours to chia seed smoothies that sustain through a long day and milkshake-style smoothies for nourishment, there's a recipe for every occasion.

Green Apple Almond Smoothie, page 32

GREEN ENERGY SMOOTHIES

Serves: 2
Prep time: 5 minutes
Storage: Best eaten immediately or consumed within 24 hours

Leafy greens are, calorie for calorie, the most concentrated source of nutrition on the planet. When you toss a handful into your liquidizer first thing in the morning, you'll get chlorophyll, antioxidants, plus a big dose of phytonutrients (plant vitamins and minerals) … all before 9 A.M!

GREEN APPLE ALMOND SMOOTHIE

Ingredients
240 ml (8½ fl oz) unsweetened almond milk
60 g (2½ oz) spinach
1 medium-sized green apple, sliced and cored
1 medium banana, sliced and frozen
1 tablespoon almond butter
2 tablespoons rolled oats
¼ – ½ tablespoon ground cinnamon
pinch of sea salt

Enjoy the sweet taste of apple pie along with a boost of health benefits from the anti-inflammatory spices, heart-healthy fat and sneaky greens. The almond butter makes this smoothie a good source of vitamin E. My personal favourite.

Calories: **191** Total fat: **6 g** Saturated fat: **1 g** Total carbohydrate: **33 g**
Dietary fibre: **6 g** Sugars: **17 g** Protein: **5 g**

1   Place the almond milk and spinach in a high-speed liquidizer and combine. Add the remaining ingredients and blend again until smooth.

TROPICAL GREEN BLISS SMOOTHIE

Ingredients
240 ml (8½ fl oz) coconut milk
60 g (2½ oz) spinach
100 g (3½ oz) pineapple (use frozen for a thicker consistency)
½ orange, squeezed (about 2 tablespoons juice)
1 medium banana, sliced and frozen
2 tablespoons hemp seeds
pinch of sea salt

Escape to the tropics with this nut-free, hemp seed-powered smoothie. Hemp seeds are an excellent source of plant-based protein and contain all nine essential amino acids.

Calories: **174** Total fat: **7 g** Saturated fat: **3 g** Total carbohydrate: **25 g**
Dietary fibre: **4 g** Sugars: **14 g** Protein: **5 g**

1   Place all the ingredients in a high-speed liquidizer, reserving a small amount of hemp seeds and blend until smooth. Sprinkle the remaining seeds on top of the smoothie before serving.

 Try This

Protein Boost for Green Apple Almond Smoothie
For an easy protein boost, top with some sliced almonds.

Ingredients

240 ml (8½ fl oz) unsweetened almond milk

60 g (2½ oz) spinach

1 tablespoon chia seeds

200 g (7 oz) frozen peaches

½ avocado

pinch of sea salt

¼ teaspoon ground cardamom

Ingredients

175 ml (6 fl oz) unsweetened cashew milk

75 g (3 oz) kale

2 tablespoons fresh mint, plus a few extra leaves for garnish

1 large banana, sliced and frozen

1 tablespoon cashew butter

pinch of sea salt

1 tablespoon cacao nibs, plus extra for garnish (optional)

Ingredients

240 ml (8½ fl oz) unsweetened cashew milk (hemp milk works well too)

60 g (2½ oz) kale

1 pear, sliced and frozen

½ avocado

2.5 cm (1 in) piece fresh ginger, peeled (½ teaspoon ground ginger)

1 teaspoon lemon juice

1 pitted Medjool date

1 tablespoon hemp seeds

PEACHY GREEN SMOOTHIE

This green smoothie is light, flavourful and creamy (thanks to the avocado) and perfect for those slower-paced days.

Calories: **143** Total fat: **9 g** Saturated fat: **1 g** Total carbohydrate: **12 g** Dietary fibre: **5 g** Sugars: **7 g** Protein: **4 g**

1 Blend all the ingredients, except the cardamom, in a high-speed liquidizer. Once combined, add the cardamom and blend again for a few seconds.

MINTY CHIP SMOOTHIE

Double up the antioxidants and energy with raw cacao added to the mix.

Calories: **152** Total fat: **6 g** Saturated fat: **1 g** Total carbohydrate: **23 g** Dietary fibre: **4 g** Sugars: **9 g** Protein: **4 g**

1 Place all the ingredients, except the cacao nibs, in a high-speed liquidizer and mix together. Once mixed, add in the cacao nibs and blend for another 10 seconds.

2 Pour into a tall glass and garnish with fresh mint leaves and a sprinkling of cacao nibs if desired.

CREAMY GINGER PEAR SMOOTHIE

Omega-rich hemp seeds, creamy avocado, energizing dates and warming ginger all meld together to create a satisfying and slow-release energizing smoothie.

Calories: **207** Total fat: **10 g** Saturated fat: **1 g** Total carbohydrate: **29 g** Dietary fibre: **6 g** Sugars: **16 g** Protein: **5 g**

1 Blend the cashew milk and kale in a high-speed liquidizer until smooth. Add the remaining ingredients and blend until combined. Enjoy!

 Cook's Notes

Extra-creamy Minty Chip Smoothie
For additional creaminess and healthy fat, add in a quarter of an avocado – that's the way I make it!

Creamy Ginger Pear Smoothie Perfection
For the sweetest flavour, it's best to use ripened pears.

BERRY-LICIOUS SMOOTHIES

Serves: 2
Prep time: 5 minutes
Storage: Best eaten immediately or consumed within 24 hours

Aside from their delicious flavour, berries are nutrition superstars – high in antioxidants and low on the glycemic index. Load up your freezer with frozen organic berries so that you can quickly blend a pretty pink, red or purple-hued smoothie without having to rush to the shop or farmers' market.

Pretty in Pink
Raspberry
Tahini Smoothie,
page 35

Blueberry Blast Smoothie,
page 35

Pumpkin Pie Smoothie,
page 36

Ingredients

240 ml (8½ fl oz) unsweetened almond milk

1 banana, sliced and frozen

125 g (4½ oz) frozen raspberries

1 tablespoon tahini, plus extra to drizzle

1 tablespoon lemon juice

½–1 teaspoon grated lemon zest

pinch of sea salt

PRETTY IN PINK RASPBERRY TAHINI SMOOTHIE

Mix these lower-glycemic gems with healing spices and nuts, and you have a heart-healthy, fibre-rich and antioxidant-filled glass of energy.

Calories: **167** Total fat: **8 g** Saturated fat: **1 g** Total carbohydrate: **23 g**
Dietary fibre: **8 g** Sugars: **10 g** Protein: **4 g**

1 Blend all the ingredients in a high-speed liquidizer until smooth. Drizzle with a touch of tahini after pouring into a glass.

Ingredients

240 ml (8½ fl oz) unsweetened almond milk (hemp milk works well for a nut-free option)

150 g (5 oz) frozen blueberries

½ avocado

1 teaspoon lemon juice

2 pitted Medjool dates

2 tablespoons hemp seeds

pinch of sea salt

BLUEBERRY BLAST SMOOTHIE

Blueberries, avocado, dates and hemp seeds combine to create an energizing and nutrient-dense smoothie.

Calories: **243** Total fat: **12 g** Saturated fat: **1 g** Total carbohydrate: **32 g**
Dietary fibre: **5 g** Sugars: **24 g** Protein: **6 g**

1 Blend all the ingredients in a high-speed liquidizer until smooth and creamy.

Ingredients

1 small beetroot, chopped (see Cook's Note below)

240 ml (8½ fl oz) unsweetened almond milk (hemp milk works well too)

225 g (8 oz) frozen pitted cherries

½ banana, sliced and frozen

½ teaspoon pure vanilla extract

½ orange, squeezed (about 2 tablespoons juice)

1 teaspoon grated orange zest

pinch of sea salt

2 tablespoons sliced almonds

ZESTY ORANGE CHERRY BEETROOT SMOOTHIE

With beetroot as a concentrated source of natural energy and cherries to improve muscle recovery, this smoothie will make you want to go-go-go.

Calories: **166** Total fat: **5 g** Saturated fat: **0 g** Total carbohydrate: **25 g**
Dietary fibre: **5 g** Sugars: **17 g** Protein: **4 g**

1 Blend the beetroot with the almond milk in a high-speed liquidizer until well combined. Mix in the remaining ingredients, reserving a few sliced almonds. Blend well. Sprinkle the remaining almond slices on top to serve.

 Cook's Note

How to Prepare and Cook Beetroot
To ensure a smooth consistency, grate or dice the raw beetroot before placing in the liquidizer.

For a milder flavour, steam or roast the beetroot in advance and allow to cool before adding to your smoothie.

Ingredients

240 ml (8½ fl oz) unsweetened almond milk (or coconut milk for a nut-free version)

125 g (4½ oz) frozen raspberries

1 banana, sliced and frozen

1 tablespoon cocoa powder or cacao powder

2 tablespoons hemp seeds

½ teaspoon pure vanilla extract

pinch of sea salt

cacao nibs or chocolate shavings, for garnish (optional)

Serves: 2

Prep time: 5 minutes

Storage: Best eaten immediately or consumed within 24 hours

RED VELVET SMOOTHIE

When those chocolate cravings hit and you need a natural energy boost, toss mood-enhancing cacao in with carb-rich and serotonin-packed bananas and berries.

Calories: **174** Total fat: **6 g** Saturated fat: **1 g** Total carbohydrate: **24 g** Dietary fibre: **8 g** Sugars: **11 g** Protein: **6 g**

1 Blend all the ingredients in a high-speed liquidizer until smooth. Pour into a glass and top with cacao nibs or chocolate shavings, if desired, for an extra boost of energy.

ORANGE IS THE NEW GREEN

Filled with fibre and healthy fats to keep your blood sugar stable, plus a big old dose of beta-carotene, orange-hued smoothies are hard to beat. The pumpkins, sweet potatoes and mangoes will give you a burst of energy from good-for-you carbs that can rival any cup of coffee, while the anti-inflammatory spices are the icing on the nutritional cake.

Ingredients

175 ml (6 fl oz) unsweetened almond milk

110 g (4 oz) unsweetened pumpkin purée (fresh or tinned)

1 tablespoon almond butter

1 pitted Medjool date

1 banana, sliced and frozen

2.5 cm (1 in) piece fresh ginger, peeled

¼ teaspoon ground cinnamon

ground nutmeg, to taste

PUMPKIN PIE SMOOTHIE

Although you can enjoy it year-round, this smoothie is an excellent precursor to winter with the warming and anti-inflammatory properties of cinnamon, ginger and nutmeg, and a dose of vitamin A.

Calories: **176** Total fat: **5 g** Saturated fat: **1 g** Total carbohydrate: **31 g** Dietary fibre: **5 g** Sugars: **18 g** Protein: **4 g**

1 Blend all the ingredients in a high-speed liquidizer until smooth.

 Try This

Top for an Energy Boost
Top your Pumpkin Pie Smoothie with some Vanilla Maple Crunch Granola (see page 85) or Buckwheat Crunchy Granola (see page 85) for an extra boost of energy.

Ingredients

175 ml (6 fl oz) unsweetened almond milk

25 g (1 oz) spinach

110 g (4 oz) unsweetened pumpkin purée (fresh or tinned)

1 tablespoon almond butter

1 pitted Medjool date

1 banana, sliced and frozen

2.5 cm (1 in) piece fresh ginger, peeled

¼ teaspoon ground cinnamon, plus extra to top

ground nutmeg, to taste

Ingredients

240 ml (8½ fl oz) cashew milk (or hemp or coconut milk for a nut-free option)

110 g (4 oz) cooked and chilled sweet potato, skin removed

2 tablespoons ground flax seeds

1 banana, sliced and frozen

1 teaspoon pure vanilla extract

¼ teaspoon ground cinnamon

ground nutmeg, to taste

pinch of sea salt

juice of 1 orange

Ingredients

240 ml (8½ fl oz) coconut milk

110 g (4 oz) frozen pineapple

75 g (3 oz) frozen mango

½ teaspoon grated fresh ginger

1 tablespoon lemon juice

1 teaspoon grated lemon zest

1 tablespoon coconut butter

1 tablespoon chia seeds, reserving some to sprinkle on top

1 tablespoon hemp seeds

2 teaspoons freshly grated turmeric

pinch of sea salt

1 macadamia nut, chopped

GREEN PUMPKIN PIE SMOOTHIE

You'll get extra micronutrients from the greens that take this orange smoothie in disguise to new heights.

Calories: **179** Total fat: **5 g** Saturated fat: **1 g** Total carbohydrate: **32 g** Dietary fibre: **5 g** Sugars: **18 g** Protein: **5 g**

1 Blend the almond milk and spinach in a high-speed liquidizer until combined. Add the remaining ingredients and blend until smooth. Sprinkle with cinnamon for a little extra spice.

SWEET POTATO POWER SMOOTHIE

Who needs energy drinks when you can load up on good-for-you-carbs and vitamin A with this creamy sweet potato smoothie?

Calories: **171** Total fat: **4 g** Saturated fat: **0 g** Total carbohydrate: **31 g** Dietary fibre: **5 g** Sugars: **15 g** Protein: **3 g**

1 Place all the ingredients, except the orange juice, in a high-speed liquidizer and blend until smooth. Squeeze in the orange juice and blend for an additional 10 seconds.

TROPICAL TURMERIC SMOOTHIE

With curcumin as turmeric's most active ingredient, it's a powerful anti-inflammatory that can help reduce aches and pains.

Calories: **145** Total fat: **7 g** Saturated fat: **2 g** Total carbohydrate: **17 g** Dietary fibre: **3 g** Sugars: **12 g** Protein: **4 g**

1 Blend all the ingredients, except the reserved chia seeds and the macadamia nut, in a high-speed liquidizer until mixed. Top with the macadamia nut for additional protein (and flavour) and the reserved chia seeds.

SMOOTHIE BOWLS

While I love sipping my smoothies, there are times when I need to dig in with a spoon and *eat* to feel fully satiated. Introducing the smoothie bowl: the same nutrition as traditional smoothies but thicker in consistency with the addition of fun toppings.

Serves: 1
Prep time: 5–10 minutes
Storage: Best eaten immediately

Ingredients

60 g (2½ oz) leafy greens (spinach, kale, romaine lettuce, Swiss chard)

175 ml (6 fl oz) plant-based milk (almond, coconut, cashew)

¼ avocado

1 banana, sliced and frozen

pinch of sea salt

¼ teaspoon each of pure vanilla extract, ground cinnamon, grated lemon zest, ground ginger, fresh mint (optional flavourings)

toppings of choice (see Toppings panel, page 73)

EASY GREEN SMOOTHIE BOWL

Start out with this basic green recipe and then customize to suit your needs. Top with a variety of nutritional boosts and create different combinations to keep you going all day long.

Calories: **203** Total fat: **8 g** Saturated fat: **1 g** Total carbohydrate: **32 g** Dietary fibre: **6 g** Sugars: **15 g** Protein: **4 g**

1 Blend the greens and plant-based milk in a high-speed liquidizer until mixed. Add the remaining ingredients, including the flavouring of choice, and blend until smooth.

2 Transfer the thick smoothie to a bowl and sprinkle with your toppings of choice – make sure to include some protein and other nutritional boosts for balanced combinations. Get creative and have fun!

Opposite: Easy Green Smoothie Bowl

 Try This

Smoothie Bowl Variations
You can use any of the smoothies from page 32 to page 50 to create a smoothie bowl; simply use a little less liquid.

RAMP-IT-UP SMOOTHIES

Serves: 2
Prep time: 5 minutes
Storage: Drink immediately

Long days and intense workouts call for smoothies that will give you enough energy to keep on going. Added bonus: these nutrient-dense and filling smoothies taste like the creamiest and most sinful milkshake.

Ingredients

175 ml (6 fl oz) unsweetened almond milk (use less for a thicker consistency)

1 tablespoon cacao powder or unsweetened cocoa powder

1 tablespoon almond butter

1½ bananas, sliced and frozen

½ teaspoon pure vanilla extract

pinch of sea salt

1 teaspoon cacao nibs

ABC SMOOTHIE

My teenage son Daniel drinks this smoothie after a day out on the lacrosse field or whenever he needs an extra boost of energy.

Calories: **158** Total fat: **7 g** Saturated fat: **1 g** Total carbohydrate: **25 g**
Dietary fibre: **4 g** Sugars: **11 g** Protein: **4 g**

1   Place all the ingredients, except the cacao nibs, in a high-speed liquidizer. Blend until smooth and creamy, pour into a glass, and sprinkle cacao nibs on top.

Ingredients

240 ml (8½ fl oz) unsweetened hemp milk

1 banana, sliced and frozen

1 tablespoon sunflower seed butter

150 g (5 oz) frozen blueberries

½ teaspoon pure vanilla extract

pinch of sea salt

1 teaspoon hemp seeds (optional)

BLUEBERRY HEMP SMOOTHIE

Enjoy the boost of protein plus omega-3s from the hemp milk in this nut-free pretty purple and creamy smoothie.

Calories: **177** Total fat: **7 g** Saturated fat: **1 g** Total carbohydrate: **26 g**
Dietary fibre: **4 g** Sugars: **15 g** Protein: **4 g**

1   Blend all the ingredients in a high-speed liquidizer until smooth and creamy. Sprinkle hemp seeds on top, if desired.

 Try This

ABC Smoothie Topping
Top the ABC Smoothie with dark chocolate shavings for an extra-decadent smoothie.

Thicker Smoothie
Add ice or extra frozen banana for a thicker smoothie.

Opposite: ABC Smoothie

Ingredients

175 ml (6 fl oz) Spiced Brazil Nut Milk (page 164)

1 tablespoon cashew butter

1 banana, sliced and frozen

1 tablespoon ground flax seeds

pinch of sea salt

VANILLA SPICE SMOOTHIE

Zippy spices make this smoothie anything but plain. Plus, you'll get your daily dose of selenium thanks to the Brazil nut milk.

Calories: **147** Total fat: **8 g** Saturated fat: **1 g** Total carbohydrate: **19 g**
Dietary fibre: **3 g** Sugars: **8 g** Protein: **3 g**

1   Blend all the ingredients in a high-speed liquidizer until smooth and creamy.

Ingredients

240 ml (8½ fl oz) unsweetened almond milk

1 tablespoon unsweetened natural peanut butter

1 banana, sliced and frozen

150 g (5 oz) frozen strawberries

½ teaspoon pure vanilla extract

pinch of sea salt

PB AND J SMOOTHIE

Reminiscent of an American peanut butter and jelly sandwich, this smoothie could become your favourite comfort food.

Calories: **139** Total fat: **6 g** Saturated fat: **1 g** Total carbohydrate: **21 g**
Dietary fibre: **4 g** Sugars: **11 g** Protein: **4 g**

1   Blend all the ingredients in a high-speed liquidizer until smooth and creamy.

Ingredients

175 ml (6 fl oz) unsweetened hemp milk (sunflower or flax milk also works)

1 tablespoon sunflower seed butter

1 banana, sliced and frozen

150 g (5 oz) frozen strawberries

½ teaspoon pure vanilla extract

pinch of sea salt

hemp seeds, for garnish (optional)

NUT-FREE PB AND J SMOOTHIE

Enjoy the same peanut butter and jelly taste sensation but in a nut-free version made with sunflower seed butter.

Calories: **144** Total fat: **8 g** Saturated fat: **4 g** Total carbohydrate: **15 g**
Dietary fibre: **2 g** Sugars: **3 g** Protein: **4 g**

1   Blend all the ingredients in a high-speed liquidizer until smooth and creamy. Garnish with hemp seeds, if desired, for a nutritional boost.

 Try This

Vanilla Spice Smoothie Milk Alternative
Instead of using Spiced Brazil Nut Milk for the Vanilla Spice Smoothie, use any plant-based milk and simply add a dash of cinnamon, ginger, ground cardamom and nutmeg (or any combination of the spices) to the liquidizer.

CHIA SMOOTHIES

Serves: 2
Prep time: 25 minutes
Storage: Drink immediately or store in the fridge for up to 24 hours

Just add water and watch them grow! Soaking two tablespoons of chia seeds will give some extra hydration plus protein, fibre, omega-3s and micronutrients to your smoothie. Chia is also an excellent source of calcium to help support bone health.

Ingredients

2 tablespoons chia seeds

240 ml (8½ fl oz) unsweetened almond milk

2 tablespoons raw almonds, soaked

100 g (3½ oz) frozen blackberries

100 g (3½ oz) frozen raspberries

1 banana, sliced and frozen

1 tablespoon lemon juice

pinch of sea salt

½ teaspoon lemon zest, plus extra for garnish

BERRY CHIA ALMOND SMOOTHIE

Double up on healthy fat from both chia seeds and almonds, along with a serving of fibre from the antioxidant-rich berries for a delicious and filling smoothie.

Calories: **200** Total fat: **8 g** Saturated fat: **0 g** Total carbohydrate: **26 g** Dietary fibre: **9 g** Sugars: **12 g** Protein: **5 g**

1 Soak the chia seeds in the almond milk for at least 20 minutes to form a gel-like consistency.

2 Before adding the other ingredients, blend the raw almonds, chia seeds and almond milk for 1 minute in a high-speed liquidizer. Add the remaining ingredients and blend until smooth and creamy. Top with additional lemon zest.

Ingredients

2 tablespoons chia seeds

240 ml (8½ fl oz) coconut milk

2 handfuls spinach

110 g (4 oz) frozen mango

1 banana, sliced and frozen

1 tablespoon sunflower seed butter

pinch of sea salt

SUNSHINE SMOOTHIE

This bright drink delivers a powerful anti-inflammatory punch with the combination of chia seeds and spinach.

Calories: **225** Total fat: **10 g** Saturated fat: **3 g** Total carbohydrate: **28 g** Dietary fibre: **5 g** Sugars: **16 g** Protein: **6 g**

1 Soak the chia seeds in the coconut milk for at least 20 minutes to form a gel-like consistency.

2 Blend the chia seeds and coconut milk in a high-speed liquidizer for 1 minute. Once combined, add the spinach and mix well. Add the remaining ingredients and blend until smooth and creamy.

 Try This

Mix up Your Berry Chia Almond Smoothie
You can mix and match any berries for the Berry Chia Almond Smoothie. Try using all blackberries and adding orange in place of the lemon. Yum!

SLUSHY SMOOTHIES

Serves: 2
Prep time: 5 minutes
Storage: Drink immediately

This hydrating smoothie is just what you need after a long run or sweaty yoga class. Whenever you need some quick energy and hydration, try these light smoothies that will remind you of your favourite refreshing slushy.

Ingredients
300 g (10½ oz) chopped watermelon
225 g (8 oz) frozen strawberries
2 tablespoons lime juice
1 teaspoon grated lime zest
pinch of sea salt
2 tablespoons fresh mint leaves

WATERMELON MINT SMOOTHIE

What better way to quench your thirst on a hot summer day than with a hydrating, rejuvenating and cooling watermelon slushy?

Calories: **92** Total fat: **0 g** Saturated fat: **0 g** Total carbohydrate: **23 g** Dietary fibre: **3 g** Sugars: **15 g** Protein: **1 g**

1   Place the watermelon in a liquidizer and mix until liquefied. Add the strawberries and lime juice and blend until smooth.

2   Add the lime zest, a pinch of salt and mint and blend just enough to mix in the leaves, while still leaving flecks throughout.

Ingredients
240 ml (8½ fl oz) coconut water
225 g (8 oz) frozen mixed berries
2 tablespoons lemon juice
1 cm (½ in) piece fresh ginger, peeled
2 tablespoons coconut flakes
1 teaspoon grated lemon zest
pinch of sea salt

MIXED BERRY AND COCONUT SLUSHY

A tasty way to restore those electrolytes and load up on antioxidants. Fresh ginger gives an extra anti-inflammatory kick.

Calories: **100** Total fat: **2 g** Saturated fat: **2 g** Total carbohydrate: **22 g** Dietary fibre: **4 g** Sugars: **13 g** Protein: **1 g**

1   Place all the ingredients in a liquidizer and blend into a slushy consistency. Enjoy immediately.

Ingredients
1 cucumber, peeled (about 320 g/11 oz)
240 ml (8½ fl oz) coconut water
200 g (7 oz) frozen pineapple
pinch of sea salt
2 tablespoons fresh mint leaves

PINEAPPLE, CUCUMBER AND COCONUT SMOOTHIE

A hydration superstar! Cucumber, pineapple and coconut combine to create a nourishing and flavourful smoothie.

Calories: **103** Total fat: **0 g** Saturated fat: **0 g** Total carbohydrate: **24 g** Dietary fibre: **2 g** Sugars: **17 g** Protein: **1 g**

1   Place the cucumber and coconut water in a liquidizer and mix until liquefied. Add the remaining ingredients, except the mint leaves, and blend until smooth.

2   Add the mint and blend just enough to mix in the leaves, while still leaving flecks throughout.

Ingredients

60 g (2½ oz) spinach

240 ml (8½ fl oz) coconut water

225 g (8 oz) frozen mango

2 tablespoons lime juice

1 teaspoon grated lime zest

1 cm (½ in) piece fresh ginger, peeled (optional)

pinch of sea salt

MANGO REFRESHER SLUSHY

Whenever I'm introducing people to the world of green smoothies, I start with the mango and spinach combination. Sweet and creamy mango masks any trace of spinach flavour.

Calories: **105** Total fat: **0 g** Saturated fat: **0 g** Total carbohydrate: **44 g**
Dietary fibre: **5 g** Sugars: **37 g** Protein: **2 g**

1   Place the spinach and coconut water in a high-speed liquidizer and mix until the greens are blended. Add the remaining ingredients and blend until smooth.

VEGGIE SMOOTHIE

Serves: 2
Prep time: 5 minutes
Storage: Best consumed immediately

With all the vegetables of the savoury blended soups and just as much hydration as the slushy smoothies, this veggie-filled option will take your green smoothie to the next level. Load up your liquidizer with mostly greens for a tasty way to flood your body with plant-based nutrients.

Ingredients

120–240 ml (4–8½ fl oz) water

75 g (3 oz) kale (can use spinach or any combination of leafy greens)

215 g (7½ oz) cucumber, peeled and roughly chopped

2 celery stalks, roughly chopped

3 romaine lettuce leaves

1 cm (½ in) piece fresh ginger, peeled (or more if preferred)

1 cm (½ in) piece fresh turmeric, peeled

2 tablespoons chopped fresh parsley

2 tablespoons lemon juice

pinch of sea salt

125 g (4½ oz) frozen pineapple chunks

1 pear, cored and roughly chopped

VEG-OUT GREEN SMOOTHIE

The pear and pineapple add sweetness, while the array of vegetables will have you meeting your five-a-day in no time.

Calories: **155** Total fat: **1 g** Saturated fat: **0 g** Total carbohydrate: **37 g**
Dietary fibre: **8 g** Sugars: **19 g** Protein: **4 g**

1   Place the water (start with 120 ml/4 fl oz) and add more for your desired consistency) and kale in a high-speed liquidizer and blend until smooth.

2   Add the cucumber, celery and lettuce leaves and continue to blend. Gradually mix in the remaining ingredients, reserving the pineapple and pear for last. Add more water if necessary and blend for a creamy and refreshing green smoothie. Serve immediately.

 Try This

Extra-hydrating Smoothie
For an extra-hydrating Veg-Out Green Smoothie, use coconut water in place of water.

BLENDED SOUPS

Serves: 2
Prep time: 10 minutes, plus
30 minutes–1 hour chilling
Storage: Consume immediately or
within 24 hours

These savoury creations are designed for busy people who love soups but don't have the time to wait for a pot to simmer and stew all day. Pair these blended soups with any of the whole food crackers, roasted chickpeas or spiced nuts to make a more substantial and balanced meal or snack.

Spicy Cucumber Soup, page 47

Moroccan Spiced Tomato Soup, page 48

Ingredients

320 g (11 oz) cucumber, peeled and roughly chopped, plus extra cubed cucumber to serve

120 ml (4 fl oz) water

½ avocado

1 tablespoon lemon juice (add more for a stronger lemon flavour)

½ teaspoon sea salt

1 teaspoon apple cider vinegar

¼–½ jalapeño pepper, seeds removed

1 spring onion

2 celery stalks

10 g (½ oz) fresh parsley

sea salt and freshly ground black pepper, to taste

SPICY CUCUMBER SOUP

Chill out on a hectic day with this spicy but refreshing soup. The jalapeño pepper and lemon juice offer just enough zing when combined with extra-hydrating cucumbers.

Calories: **92** Total fat: **6 g** Saturated fat: **1 g** Total carbohydrate: **8 g**
Dietary fibre: **4 g** Sugars: **3 g** Protein: **3 g**

1   Place the cucumber and water in a liquidizer and combine until almost smooth. Scrape down the sides.

2   Add the remaining ingredients and blend until the vegetables are incorporated and smooth. Add seasonings to taste.

3   Check the consistency of your savoury soup, as this can vary depending on your ingredients. If the smoothie is too thick, add extra water (up to 120 ml/4 fl oz should work) to thin.

4   Chill for 20–30 minutes for the best flavour. Serve with fresh cucumber cubes on top and a side of Whole Food Crackers (see page 92).

Ingredients

25 g (1 oz) spinach

120–175 ml (4–6 fl oz) water

1 small courgette, chopped

½ avocado

2 celery stalks

1–2 tablespoons chopped onion

½–1 small garlic clove

2 tablespoons lime juice (or lemon juice)

½ teaspoon sea salt

10 g (½ oz) fresh parsley

10 g (½ oz) fresh coriander

any combination of chopped red pepper, sliced cucumber and hemp seeds, for garnish

CREAMY GREEN SOUP

This creamy soup is an excellent way to get instant nourishment. Blending the greens helps break down the tough cell membranes so that you start energizing your body from the very first spoonful.

Calories: **98** Total fat: **6 g** Saturated fat: **1 g** Total carbohydrate: **10 g**
Dietary fibre: **4 g** Sugars: **3 g** Protein: **3 g**

1   In a high-speed liquidizer, blend the spinach and 120 ml (4 fl oz) of the water until smooth.

2   Add the remaining ingredients, except the parsley and coriander, and blend to combine. Mix in the herbs and blend again for 10–20 seconds. Add more water if necessary for the desired consistency.

3   Top with chopped red peppers, cucumber or hemp seeds, then serve immediately or chill in the fridge for 1 hour. Enjoy with Whole Food Crackers (see page 92).

🥄 **Try This**

Refrigerating Soups
The soups will thicken if refrigerated overnight. Adjust the consistency by adding 1–2 tablespoons of water.

Protein Boost
Add 1–2 tablespoons of raw cashews that have been soaked for 1–2 hours to your Creamy Green Soup for added protein.

Ingredients

2 garlic cloves, minced

1 teaspoon paprika

1 teaspoon ground cumin

pinch of cayenne pepper (add more if you like heat)

1 tablespoon olive oil, plus extra to drizzle

540 g (1¼ lb) tomatoes, roughly chopped

1 tablespoon white wine vinegar

½ teaspoon sea salt

2 tablespoons water

10 g (⅓ oz) fresh coriander, plus extra, chopped, for garnish

sea salt and freshly ground black pepper, to taste

MOROCCAN SPICED TOMATO SOUP

Refreshing and flavourful, this chilled Moroccan spiced soup boasts health benefits due to the anti-inflammatory spices plus the huge dose of lycopene from the fresh tomatoes.

Calories: **122** Total fat: **8 g** Saturated fat: **1 g** Total carbohydrate: **13 g**
Dietary fibre: **4 g** Sugars: **7 g** Protein: **3 g**

1   Combine the garlic, paprika, cumin, cayenne and olive oil in a small frying pan. Cook over a low heat, stirring constantly, for 2 minutes. Remove from the heat and let cool.

2   Place the tomatoes in a food processor and process, leaving some small chunks of tomato. Add the cooled spice mixture, vinegar, salt and water, and pulse until combined but not completely smooth. Add the coriander and pulse 10–12 times. Refrigerate until cold.

3   Garnish with chopped coriander and a drizzle of olive oil. Serve with Roasted Chickpeas (see page 108) or any of the Whole Food Crackers (see page 92).

Ingredients

1½ tablespoons olive oil

1 garlic clove, minced

40 g (1½ oz) onion, diced

1–2.5 cm (½–1 in) piece fresh ginger, peeled and grated, to taste

1 cm (½ in) piece fresh turmeric, peeled and grated

390 g (14 oz) carrots, peeled and sliced in rounds

¼ teaspoon sea salt

480 ml (17 fl oz) low-sodium vegetable broth (if not using low sodium, then omit the salt)

240 ml (8½ fl oz) water

fresh parsley, for garnish

freshly ground black pepper, to taste

CARROT GINGER SOUP

Give yourself a hug from the inside out with the vitamin A and healing ginger and turmeric in this delicious soup.

Calories: **177** Total fat: **7 g** Saturated fat: **1 g** Total carbohydrate: **26 g**
Dietary fibre: **6 g** Sugars: **12 g** Protein: **2 g**

1   Heat 1 tablespoon of the olive oil in a medium saucepan over medium heat. Add the garlic, onion and ginger, and cook for about 1 minute until the mixture begins to sweat. Add the remaining olive oil and the turmeric, carrots and salt. Cook for about 2 minutes or less, stirring continuously.

2   Add the vegetable broth plus 120 ml (4 fl oz) of the water and bring to a boil. Reduce to low and let simmer for 25 minutes until the carrots can be easily pierced with a fork. Remove from the heat and let cool to a lukewarm temperature.

3   Purée in a liquidizer and add the remaining water (or more if needed) to blend into a smooth and silky consistency.

4   Garnish with chopped parsley and serve with Whole Food Crackers (see page 92). Enjoy hot or cold.

Try This

Protein Topping
Top your Blended Soups with Roasted Chickpeas (see page 108) for crunch and extra plant-based protein.

ICE CREAM SMOOTHIES

Serves: 4
Prep time: 5 minutes
Storage: Eat immediately

Not to be sneaky, but there are hidden veggies in all of these smoothies. The ice cream-style smoothie creations are all thick and filling, and taste like a flavourful soft-serve ice cream. Pull out a spoon and divvy it up with everyone at the table. A little goes a long way.

COOKIE DOUGH SMOOTHIE

Ingredients
1 medium courgette, peeled and roughly chopped

175 ml (6 fl oz) coconut milk

1½ bananas, sliced and frozen

2 pitted Medjool dates

1 tablespoon cashew butter

½ teaspoon ground cinnamon, plus extra to serve

1 teaspoon pure vanilla extract

50 g (2 oz) rolled oats, plus extra to serve

pinch of sea salt

1 tablespoon cacao nibs, plus extra to serve

With all the flavours of cookie dough but none of the sugar and flour, this smoothie is too good to be true. Nobody will ever suspect the hidden courgette.

Calories: **147** Total fat: **3 g** Saturated fat: **1 g** Total carbohydrate: **27 g**
Dietary fibre: **3 g** Sugars: **15 g** Protein: **3 g**

1 Place the courgette and coconut milk in a liquidizer and mix until smooth. Add the remaining ingredients, except the cacao nibs. Blend until well combined and creamy.

2 Once combined, add the cacao nibs and pulse for a few seconds.

3 Top with a sprinkling of cacao nibs, cinnamon and oats. Serve in small glasses for a filling and nourishing dessert.

CHERRY CHOCOLATE BOMB SMOOTHIE

Ingredients
240 ml (8½ fl oz) coconut milk (or unsweetened almond milk)

60 g (2½ oz) fresh spinach

250 g (9 oz) pitted frozen cherries

2 bananas, sliced and frozen

1 teaspoon pure vanilla extract

2 tablespoons cacao powder

pinch of sea salt

cacao nibs or a sprinkling of chocolate chips, to serve

Just thinking about the combination of cherries and chocolate is enough to lift your mood and your energy levels. You can't taste the spinach.

Calories: **104** Total fat: **1 g** Saturated fat: **0 g** Total carbohydrate: **23 g**
Dietary fibre: **4 g** Sugars: **18 g** Protein: **3 g**

1 Place the coconut milk and spinach in a liquidizer and mix until smooth.

2 Add the remaining ingredients and blend into a thick and soft-serve ice cream consistency. Top with cacao nibs and serve immediately.

Ingredients

60 g (2½ oz) spinach

240 ml (8½ fl oz) unsweetened
almond or coconut milk

1 ripe avocado, pitted and peeled

2 pitted Medjool dates

1 teaspoon pure vanilla extract

8 fresh mint leaves (or ½ teaspoon
mint extract)

2 large bananas, sliced and frozen

pinch of sea salt

2 tablespoons cacao nibs or
chocolate chips

additional cacao nibs, chocolate
chips, or shaved chocolate, and a
fresh mint sprig, to serve

Ingredients

175 ml (6 fl oz) unsweetened almond
milk (coconut milk works too)

110 g (4 oz) unsweetened pumpkin
purée (fresh or tinned)

1 tablespoon raw cacao powder or
unsweetened cocoa powder

2 large bananas, sliced and frozen

1 cm (½ in) piece fresh ginger,
peeled

½ teaspoon ground cinnamon, plus
extra to serve

sprinkle of ground nutmeg

2 pitted Medjool dates

1 tablespoon almond butter (cashew
butter also works)

pinch of sea salt

cacao nibs, to serve

MINT CHOCOLATE CHIP SMOOTHIE

If you loved mint chocolate chip ice cream as a kid, then
this flavourful and nutrient-dense smoothie with hidden
greens is for you.

Calories: **175** Total fat: **7 g** Saturated fat: **1 g** Total carbohydrate: **27 g**
Dietary fibre: **5 g** Sugars: **15 g** Protein: **4 g**

1 Blend the spinach and almond milk in a liquidizer until
smooth.

2 Add the remaining ingredients, except the cacao nibs, and
blend until smooth and creamy. Once combined, add the
cacao nibs and pulse for a few seconds.

3 Serve immediately with your toppings of choice.

VELVETY CHOCOLATE PUMPKIN SMOOTHIE

Chocolate and pumpkin combine for double the dose of
antioxidants and double the flavour.

Calories: **134** Total fat: **3 g** Saturated fat: **0 g** Total carbohydrate: **28 g**
Dietary fibre: **4 g** Sugars: **16 g** Protein: **3 g**

1 Place the almond milk, pumpkin purée and cocoa or cacao
powder in a liquidizer and mix until smooth.

2 Add the remaining ingredients and blend into a creamy
consistency. Top with cinnamon and/or cacao nibs.
Serve immediately.

  Cook's Note

Pumpkin Pie Spice Mix
If you don't have access to fresh ginger, cinnamon and
nutmeg, replace them with 1 teaspoon pumpkin pie spice in
the Velvety Chocolate Pumpkin Smoothie.

2

JUICES AND DRINKS

Staying hydrated is essential for your overall health and well-being. Not getting enough fluid can lead to headaches, fatigue and low energy, which doesn't work well in the midst of a busy schedule. These drinks are designed to flood your body with nutrients and support your health in multiple ways. Try the Get-Up-and-Green Juice (see page 52) for an energizing start to your day, or discover the healing powers of turmeric in your afternoon latte (see page 63).

Get-Up-and-Green Juice, page 52

GREEN JUICES

Almost like an intravenous injection of nutrients, fresh juice floods your cells and nourishes your body instantly. The chlorophyll-rich juice strengthens your immune system, controls inflammation and enhances your body's ability to carry oxygen.

Serves: 2
Prep time: 10 minutes
Storage: Best consumed immediately or within a few hours

Ingredients
3 kale leaves
2 celery stalks
1 large lemon, peeled
handful of spinach
1 medium – large apple
1 head of romaine lettuce
1 cucumber, peeled
1 cm (½ in) piece fresh ginger, peeled (optional)

GET-UP-AND-GREEN JUICE

Send love and nourishment to your cells with anti-inflammatory and alkalizing greens.

Calories: **84** Total fat: **1 g** Saturated fat: **0 g** Total carbohydrate: **27 g**
Dietary fibre: **1 g** Sugars: **13 g** Protein: **6 g**

1   Wash and chop the fruits and vegetables. Push all ingredients through a juicer.

Ingredients
3 kale leaves
2 celery stalks
1 head of romaine lettuce
1 lime, peeled
small bunch of fresh parsley
2 broccoli stalks (reserve the florets for another time)
1 ripe pear
1 cm (½ in) piece fresh ginger, peeled

SPICE-IT-UP GREEN JUICE

Pear and lime create a sweet and tangy flavour in this green juice. Broccoli adds earthy sweetness, while parsley is loaded with nutrients.

Calories: **110** Total fat: **2 g** Saturated fat: **0 g** Total carbohydrate: **34 g**
Dietary fibre: **2 g** Sugars: **12 g** Protein: **9 g**

1   Wash and chop the fruits and vegetables. Push all ingredients through a juicer.

Ingredients
4–5 kale leaves
2 celery stalks
½ cucumber
2.5 cm (1 in) piece fresh turmeric, peeled
1 cm (½ in) piece fresh ginger, peeled
125 g (4½ oz) pineapple
handful of fresh coriander
pinch of sea salt

ANTI-INFLAMMATORY GREEN JUICE

While all the green juices boast anti-inflammatory properties, this one kicks it up a notch with turmeric, ginger, coriander and pineapple all in one glass.

Calories: **63** Total fat: **1 g** Saturated fat: **0 g** Total carbohydrate: **17 g**
Dietary fibre: **1 g** Sugars: **8 g** Protein: **3 g**

1   Wash and chop the fruits and vegetables. Push all ingredients through a juicer.

Ingredients

2–3 kale leaves
2 celery stalks
1 large cucumber
1 grapefruit, peeled
½ lemon, peeled
small bunch of fresh mint
pinch of sea salt

Ingredients

2–3 broccoli stalks (reserve the florets for another time)
2 celery stalks
1 head of romaine lettuce
handful of fresh parsley
1 cucumber
2 handfuls of spinach
1 lemon, peeled
1 cm (½ in) piece fresh ginger, peeled (optional)

REFRESHING GREEN JUICE

Celery, cucumber and grapefruit combine with mint for a refreshing combination. Try using pink grapefruit for an even sweeter and stronger citrus flavour.

Calories: **60** Total fat: **1 g** Saturated fat: **1 g** Total carbohydrate: **17 g**
Dietary fibre: **1 g** Sugars: **11 g** Protein: **3 g**

1 Wash and chop the fruits and vegetables. Push all ingredients through a juicer.

RISE-AND-SHINE GREEN JUICE

Go hard-core with this lower sugar juice. Enjoy this detoxifying juice when you need to flood your body with nutrients.

Calories: **74** Total fat: **1 g** Saturated fat: **0 g** Total carbohydrate: **23 g**
Dietary fibre: **1 g** Sugars: **7 g** Protein: **8 g**

1 Wash and chop the fruits and vegetables. Push all ingredients through a juicer.

 Try This

Top for Balance
For a more balanced snack, top your juice with hemp or chia seeds or eat a handful of nuts on the side.

Right: Refreshing Green Juice

RED JUICES

Serves: 2
Prep time: 10 minutes
Storage: Best consumed immediately or within a few hours

Who needs caffeine when you can have a bolt of energy from these naturally sweet and immune-boosting vegetable juices? Beetroot is a packed with complex carbohydrates and is an excellent source of quick energy for the active lifestyle. Root vegetables are reported to help you feel grounded and centred.

Ingredients

1 beetroot

4 carrots

2 celery stalks

1 pear

1 cm (½ in) piece fresh ginger, peeled (can use up to 2.5 cm/1 in)

YOU GOT THE BEET JUICE

Drink this juice in the morning to feel vibrant, or use it as an afternoon pick-me-up before a high-powered sweat session.

Calories: **80** Total fat: **0 g** Saturated fat: **0 g** Total carbohydrate: **25 g** Dietary fibre: **1 g** Sugars: **15 g** Protein: **2 g**

1 Wash and chop the fruits and vegetables. Push all ingredients through a juicer.

Ingredients

1 beetroot

2–3 carrots

2 celery stalks

1 cucumber, peeled

1 head of romaine lettuce

handful of spinach

2 kale leaves

bunch of fresh parsley

1 lemon, peeled

pinch of sea salt

DRINK YOUR VEGGIES

With a line-up of naturally sweet vegetables and the citrus zing of lemon, this is a wonderfully energizing juice.

Calories: **98** Total fat: **2 g** Saturated fat: **0 g** Total carbohydrate: **30 g** Dietary fibre: **2 g** Sugars: **13 g** Protein: **8 g**

1 Wash and chop the fruits and vegetables. Push all ingredients through a juicer.

Ingredients

1 beetroot

3 carrots

1 orange, peeled

3 celery stalks

1 lemon, peeled

pinch of sea salt

ORANGE YOU BEET JUICE

The orange in this juice gives you an extra shot of vitamin C. Not sold on the beetroot yet? Swap it for a medium raw sweet potato for a milder flavour.

Calories: **86** Total fat: **1 g** Saturated fat: **0 g** Total carbohydrate: **27 g** Dietary fibre: **1 g** Sugars: **17 g** Protein: **4 g**

1 Wash and chop the fruits and vegetables. Push all ingredients through a juicer.

Opposite: You Got the Beet Juice

Smoothies Versus Juices

Smoothies and juices are both excellent ways to include a variety of fruits and vegetables in your diet.

What is the difference? Smoothies are made in a liquidizer and use the entire fruit and vegetable (sometimes minus the seeds and skin), meaning all the fibre is intact. In addition to the fresh produce, you can add in nuts, seeds, spices and other nutritional boosts. Because it is easy to whip up a liquidizer filled with healthy fats and proteins, a smoothie is filling and can serve as a sustained-release form of energy.

Juices are made in a juicer, where the pulp is separated from the fruits, vegetables and fresh spices. The benefit of drinking a glass of extracted juice without the fibre is that all the vitamins and minerals can go straight to your cells and flood your body with oxygen, chlorophyll and phytonutrients almost instantly. Juicing is also easy on your digestive system and offers a quick-release form of hydrating energy.

How to choose? Make room for both smoothies and juices. If you are short on time, blending is a quicker option. Opt for a juice when you want a drink that is hydrating, healing and repairing. Whip up a smoothie for a more filling option. Whether you blend or juice, you're filling your body with vibrant and colourful whole foods.

DIY ELECTROLYTE DRINKS

Serves: 2
Prep time: 5–10 minutes
Storage: Up to 1 day in the fridge

While staying hydrated is important, it is equally important to replenish your electrolytes after a sweaty workout. That's when many of us turn to the commercial sports drinks, but you can easily throw together a homemade version in no time. Not only will you leave out the unhealthy and unwanted ingredients, but you'll save some money, too!

Ingredients
480 ml (17 fl oz) filtered water
1 tablespoon maple syrup
⅛ teaspoon sea salt
55 ml (2 fl oz) lime juice
55 ml (2 fl oz) lemon juice

DIY LEMON-AID

When water just won't hit the spot, mix up a batch of this tangy drink for a quick hit of carbohydrates, sodium and potassium. Pour some into a to-go jar or bottle to sip while you sweat.

Calories: **41** Total fat: **0 g** Saturated fat: **0 g** Total carbohydrate: **12 g**
Dietary fibre: **0 g** Sugars: **8 g** Protein: **0 g**

1 Place the filtered water, maple syrup and salt in a jug and stir well. Mix in the remaining ingredients and stir again. Serve immediately or store in the fridge to enjoy for a delicious electrolyte replacement drink after a workout.

Ingredients
480 ml (17 fl oz) filtered water
1 tablespoon maple syrup
⅛ teaspoon sea salt
55 ml (2 fl oz) lime juice
55 ml (2 fl oz) lemon juice
juice of an orange or grapefruit

CITRUS-AID

Squeeze in the juice of an orange or grapefruit for some additional vitamin C and potassium.

Calories: **60** Total fat: **0 g** Saturated fat: **0 g** Total carbohydrate: **16 g**
Dietary fibre: **0 g** Sugars: **11 g** Protein: **1 g**

1 Follow the recipe for DIY Lemon-Aid (above) and squeeze in the fresh juice of an orange or grapefruit.

Ingredients
480 ml (17 fl oz) filtered water
1 tablespoon maple syrup
⅛ teaspoon sea salt
55 ml (2 fl oz) lime juice
55 ml (2 fl oz) lemon juice
6 Coconut Ice Cubes (page 152)

COCO REFRESHER

Take your DIY electrolyte replacement drink to the next level with Coconut Ice Cubes (see page 152). Double up on the minerals slushy-style by throwing the mix into the liquidizer.

Calories: **51** Total fat: **0 g** Saturated fat: **0 g** Total carbohydrate: **15 g**
Dietary fibre: **0 g** Sugars: **8 g** Protein: **0 g**

1 Follow the recipe for DIY Lemon-Aid (above) and add in about 6 Coconut Ice Cubes per serving. Either blend in the coconut cubes in a high-speed liquidizer for a slushy or use the cubes just like normal ice cubes.

Opposite: DIY Lemon-Aid

Ingredients

2 tablespoons chia seeds

480 ml (17 fl oz) filtered water

⅛ teaspoon sea salt

55 ml (2 fl oz) lime juice

55 ml (2 fl oz) lemon juice

1 tablespoon maple syrup

CHIA LEMON-AID

Because chia seeds hold up to ten times their weight in water, they add extra hydrating properties to this electrolyte replacement drink.

Calories: **75** Total fat: **3 g** Saturated fat: **0 g** Total carbohydrate: **12 g**
Dietary fibre: **3 g** Sugars: **5 g** Protein: **2 g**

1 Add the chia seeds (1 tablespoon per serving) to the water and stir, then follow the recipe for DIY Lemon-Aid (see page 56). Let the mixture thicken for about 10 minutes, continuing to stir several times. Add the juices and maple syrup and mix well.

Yield: 1 jug

Ingredients

fresh filtered water

Choose any of these great flavour combinations:

grapefruit and fresh mint

raspberry and lime

strawberry, lemon and fresh basil

cucumber, lemon and ginger

kiwi, lemon and blueberry

mixed citrus slices

watermelon, lime and fresh mint

SPA WATER

Give your plain old water a little pizazz. Try any of these combinations (or come up with your own) for a delicious healing hydrator.

1 Fill up a jug with fresh filtered water. Slice up your chosen fruits and herbs and add your combination to the jug.

🥄 **Try This**

Individual Portions
Create individual grab-and-go drinks by making your Spa Water in water bottles or mason jars.

Opposite: Spa Water variations

HEALING WARMING DRINKS

Serves: 1
Prep time: 5 minutes
Storage: Drink immediately

There's nothing more soothing to the soul than sitting down with a warm drink in hand. When your favourite mug is filled with spices and nutrients that flood your system with antioxidants and anti-inflammatory properties, it's no wonder you feel rejuvenated after just one sip.

HOT CHOCOLATE WITH A KICK

Ingredients

240 ml (8½ fl oz) unsweetened nut milk or coconut milk

1½ tablespoons cacao powder

1 tablespoon maple syrup

½ teaspoon ground cinnamon

⅛ teaspoon cayenne pepper

pinch of sea salt

Give your metabolism a boost with cayenne pepper tossed into this fragrant hot cocoa. Take a moment to sit down, relax and enjoy this deliciously decadent drink.

Calories: **125** Total fat: **4 g** Saturated fat: **2 g** Total carbohydrate: **21 g**
Dietary fibre: **3 g** Sugars: **8 g** Protein: **3 g**

1 Place the nut or coconut milk and cacao powder in a small saucepan over medium-high heat. Stir to dissolve the cacao powder.

2 Mix in the maple syrup and spices. Bring to a simmer.

3 Remove from the heat, taste and adjust the seasoning as needed. Serve in your favourite mug.

CHOCOLATE ALMOND BUTTER DELIGHT

Ingredients

240 ml (8½ fl oz) unsweetened almond milk (or any plant-based milk)

1½ tablespoons cacao powder

1 tablespoon maple syrup

½ teaspoon pure vanilla extract

pinch of sea salt

1 tablespoon almond butter

ground cinnamon, for topping (optional)

Take your hot cocoa to another level of creaminess, taste and flavour with a spoonful of satisfying almond butter.

Calories: **217** Total fat: **12 g** Saturated fat: **1 g** Total carbohydrate: **23 g**
Dietary fibre: **5 g** Sugars: **9 g** Protein: 6 g

1 Follow the basic instructions for the Hot Chocolate with a Kick (see above), adding the vanilla extract with the maple syrup. Once warmed, remove from the heat and place the warm drink and almond butter in a liquidizer for 20–30 seconds. Don't put the lid on too tightly so the steam can escape. Pour into a mug and top with cinnamon, if desired, then enjoy your creamy warming drink!

> 🥄 **Try This**
>
> **Frothy Hot Chocolate With A Kick**
> After heating the ingredients on the hob, pour the mixture into the liquidizer for 20–30 seconds. Don't put the lid on too tightly so the steam can escape. It will make the drink nice and frothy! (You can also try this with the Healing Turmeric Latte, see page 63.)

Opposite: Hot Chocolate with a Kick

Cook's Notes

Extra-creamy Healing Turmeric Latte
Use coconut butter in place of coconut oil for added creaminess.

Making Turmeric Paste
To make the paste, combine two parts turmeric powder with one part boiling water. Store in the fridge for up to 5 days.

Ingredients

240 ml (8½ fl oz) unsweetened almond milk

½ teaspoon ground cinnamon

pinch of ground nutmeg

pinch of ground cardamom

pinch of sea salt

½ teaspoon pure vanilla extract

2 teaspoons maple syrup

1 tablespoon almond butter

SPICED VANILLA ALMOND MILK

All the healing spices in one mug! Choose this super-nourishing drink when you want to show your body some extra TLC.

Calories: **169** Total fat: **11 g** Saturated fat: **1 g** Total carbohydrate: **15 g** Dietary fibre: **3 g** Sugars: **6 g** Protein: **5 g**

1 Place the almond milk, spices, vanilla and maple syrup in a small saucepan over medium-high heat. Bring to a simmer.

2 Once warmed, remove from the heat and place in a liquidizer. Add the almond butter and blend for 20–30 seconds. Don't put the lid on too tightly so the steam can escape. Pour into a mug and enjoy!

Ingredients

240 ml (8½ fl oz) unsweetened plant-based milk

1 ½ tablespoons cacao powder

1 tablespoon maple syrup (or to taste)

drop of mint extract, to taste (a little goes a long way)

pinch of sea salt

PEPPERMINT HOT CHOCOLATE

You don't need to wait for the holidays to enjoy this flavourful hot cocoa. Peppermint and chocolate are a match made in heaven.

Calories: **116** Total fat: **3 g** Saturated fat: **1 g** Total carbohydrate: **20 g** Dietary fibre: **3 g** Sugars: **8 g** Protein: **3 g**

1 Follow the recipe for Hot Chocolate with a Kick (see page 61), adding the mint extract with the maple syrup.

Ingredients

240 ml (8½ fl oz) unsweetened almond or coconut milk

1 heaping tablespoon grated fresh turmeric (or use about 2 teaspoons turmeric paste – see Cook's Note, opposite)

1 tablespoon grated fresh ginger (or 1 teaspoon ground)

1 teaspoon ground cinnamon

small pinch of freshly ground black pepper (can use whole peppercorns if using a liquidizer)

1 tablespoon coconut oil

½ teaspoon pure vanilla extract (optional)

2 teaspoons honey or maple syrup, to taste

HEALING TURMERIC LATTE

A dash of black pepper in my signature latte enhances the bioavailability of turmeric, a powerful anti-inflammatory. Take one sip, and you will be hooked.

Calories: **201** Total fat: **17 g** Saturated fat: **13 g** Total carbohydrate: **15 g** Dietary fibre: **4 g** Sugars: **11 g** Protein: **1 g**

1 Gently warm the almond or coconut milk in a small saucepan. Do not boil. Add the turmeric, ginger, cinnamon and black pepper.

2 Add the coconut oil and optional vanilla extract and heat until melted. Use a wire whisk or immersion blender to mix until frothy and heated through.

3 Stir in the honey or maple syrup to taste. Sip, savour and enjoy.

Opposite: Healing Turmeric Latte

Ingredients

340 ml (12 fl oz) hot water

2.5 cm (1 in) piece fresh ginger,
    peeled

2.5 cm (1 in) piece fresh turmeric

1 cinnamon stick

lemon or orange slices (optional)

2 teaspoons honey, or to taste

CALMING TURMERIC TEA

This turmeric tea is lighter than its latte cousin (without
the plant-based milk base), but it still delivers the same anti-
inflammatory and healing punch.

Calories: **21** Total fat: **0 g** Saturated fat: **0 g** Total carbohydrate: **6 g**
Dietary fibre: **0 g** Sugars: **6 g** Protein: **0 g**

1   Place the water, ginger, turmeric, cinnamon stick and
    orange or lemon slices, if using, in a small saucepan and
    heat. Once simmering, but not boiling, remove from
    the heat.

2   Let the tea sit for 2–3 minutes to infuse. Stir in the honey.

Ingredients

340 ml (12 fl oz) hot water

2.5 cm (1 in) piece fresh ginger,
    peeled

pinch of cayenne pepper (optional)

2 teaspoons honey, or to taste

juice of ½ a lemon (about 2
    tablespoons juice)

LEMON, GINGER AND HONEY TEA

Feeling a little run-down from your busy schedule? Steep a
hot cup of this immunity-building tea as a natural flu- and
cold-fighting remedy when your body is exhausted and more
susceptible to getting sick.

Calories: **49** Total fat: **0 g** Saturated fat: **0 g** Total carbohydrate: **14 g**
Dietary fibre: **0 g** Sugars: **12 g** Protein: **0 g**

1   Place the water, ginger and cayenne pepper, if using, in a
    small saucepan and heat. Once simmering, but not boiling,
    remove from the heat.

2   Let the mixture sit for 2–3 minutes, then stir in the honey.
    Squeeze the juice from ½ a lemon into the tea and serve
    immediately. Sip any time you feel under the weather.

 Cook's Note

Tea Infusion
You can either strain the tea through a fine-mesh strainer
or leave the spices and citrus in the bottom of the saucepan
to continue infusing.

WHOLE FOOD MORNINGS

Start each morning feeling as strong and healthy as possible. Since we don't always have time to prepare a nourishing sit-down breakfast, this chapter is filled with quick and easy options to get you ready to take on the demands of your day. Grab some overnight oats from the fridge and simply head out the door (see page 71), or help yourself to a whole food muffin baked in advance to enjoy with your morning green juice (see page 76).

Banana Chocolate Chip Baked Oat Cups, page 74

Yield: 375 g (13 oz)
Serving size: 375 g (13 oz)
Prep time: 5 minutes
Storage: Eat immediately

QUINOA BREAKFAST PORRIDGE

Naturally gluten free, quinoa contains all nine essential amino acids and is an excellent choice for adding plant-based protein to your diet. To make a warming porridge in under five minutes, precook the quinoa, then add fruit, plant-based milk and spices, and top it off with an extra nutritional boost (see Toppings panel, page 73).

Ingredients

125 g (4½ oz) cooked quinoa

120 ml (4 fl oz) unsweetened plant-based milk

½ apple, chopped but not peeled

½ teaspoon ground cinnamon, plus extra to serve

pinch of sea salt

maple syrup or honey, to taste (optional)

1 tablespoon chopped hazelnuts

APPLE, CINNAMON AND HAZELNUT CRUMBLE PORRIDGE

If you're okay with tastes and flavours reminiscent of apple pie, then this might just be your pre-workout meal of choice!

Calories: **270** Total fat: **5 g** Saturated fat: **3 g** Total carbohydrate: **39 g**
Dietary fibre: **6 g** Sugars: **7 g** Protein: **6 g**

1   Heat the cooked quinoa, plant-based milk, apple, cinnamon, salt, and maple syrup or honey, if using, in a saucepan over medium heat.

2   Once warm, place in a bowl and top with the chopped hazelnuts and some additional cinnamon. Add more plant-based milk for extra creaminess if desired.

 Cook's Note

Cook Apple Until Softened
For the Apple, Cinnamon and Hazelnut Crumble Porridge, cook the apple until softened and warmed through. If possible, use organic apples.

Right: Apple, Cinnamon and Hazelnut Crumble Porridge, served with blueberries on top

Ingredients

125 g (4½ oz) cooked quinoa

120 ml (4 fl oz) unsweetened nut milk of choice (almond works well)

½ banana, sliced

¼ teaspoon ground cinnamon

pinch of sea salt

maple syrup or honey, to taste (optional)

2 teaspoons natural unsalted peanut butter

PEANUT BUTTER AND BANANA PORRIDGE

How can you go wrong when you combine the taste (and protein) of peanut butter with the creaminess and nutrition of banana?

Calories: **298** Total fat: **9 g** Saturated fat: **1 g** Total carbohydrate: **47 g**
Dietary fibre: **7 g** Sugars: **8 g** Protein: **10 g**

1   Heat the cooked quinoa, nut milk, banana, cinnamon, salt and maple syrup or honey, if using, in a saucepan over medium heat.

2   Once warm, add the peanut butter and stir to warm through and combine. Place in a bowl and serve. Add more nut milk for extra creaminess if desired.

Ingredients

125 g (4½ oz) cooked quinoa

120 ml (4 fl oz) unsweetened coconut or almond milk (add more for a creamier consistency if needed)

¼ teaspoon ground cinnamon (or to taste)

60 g (2½ oz) fresh berries (strawberries, raspberries, blueberries, blackberries)

½ teaspoon pure vanilla extract

pinch of sea salt

maple syrup or honey, to taste (optional)

1 tablespoon sliced almonds, to top

shredded coconut, to top

BERRY, COCONUT AND ALMOND PORRIDGE

Add a splash of colour with the deeply pigmented berries to top off this nutrient-rich variation. The coconut and almonds will help stave off any hunger pangs all morning long.

Calories: **276** Total fat: **9 g** Saturated fat: **2 g** Total carbohydrate: **42 g**
Dietary fibre: **6 g** Sugars: **7 g** Protein: **8 g**

1   Heat the cooked quinoa, coconut or almond milk, cinnamon, half the berries, vanilla extract, salt and the maple syrup or honey, if using, in a saucepan over medium heat.

2   Once warmed through, place in a bowl and top with the remaining berries, shredded coconut and nuts. Add more plant-based milk for extra creaminess if desired.

 Cook's Note

How to Make Perfect Quinoa
To cook quinoa, add one part quinoa to two parts water in a small saucepan, with a pinch of salt and a drop of olive oil. Bring to a boil, then reduce to a simmer and cover for 15 minutes or until all the water is absorbed. Turn off the heat and let sit for 5 minutes before removing the lid and fluffing with a fork. For added flavour, cook the quinoa in half water and half unsweetened plant-based milk.

Store your precooked quinoa in the fridge for up to 4 days.

CHIA SEED PUDDING

Aside from being a nutritional powerhouse filled with an easily digestible form of protein and omega-3 fatty acids, chia seeds offer healthy fuel for stamina and endurance. Top your pudding with fruit or layer it into parfaits to support your energy needs.

Yield: See each recipe
Serving size: See each recipe
Prep time: 20 minutes, plus 2 hours resting
Storage: Up to 4 days in the fridge
Note: Coconut Raspberry Chia Seed Pudding should be eaten within 2 days due to the fresh raspberries

Yield: 250 g (9 oz)
Serving size: 125 g (4½ oz)

Ingredients
240 ml (8½ fl oz) unsweetened plant-based milk
40 g (1½ oz) chia seeds
1½ tablespoons maple syrup
½ teaspoon pure vanilla extract
pinch of sea salt

SIMPLE CHIA SEED PUDDING

From a satisfying breakfast to an afternoon pick-me-up or even a dessert, this versatile chia seed pudding will make its way into your nutrition repertoire in no time.

Calories: **142** Total fat: **7 g** Saturated fat: **0 g** Total carbohydrate: **11 g** Dietary fibre: **3 g** Sugars: **9 g** Protein: **4 g**

1   Pour all the ingredients into a bowl and stir until well combined. Allow the chia seeds to settle for 20 minutes, whisking every 5 minutes, until the mixture thickens. Place in the fridge and store for at least 2 hours or overnight.

2   Check for the desired thickness and flavour, adjusting if necessary. When ready to serve, spoon into bowls and top with fresh fruit. Enjoy!

Yield: 250 g (9 oz)
Serving size: 125 g (4½ oz)

Ingredients
240 ml (8½ fl oz) unsweetened plant-based milk
40 g (1½ oz) chia seeds
1½ tablespoons maple syrup
½ teaspoon pure vanilla extract
pinch of sea salt
1–2 teaspoons grated lemon zest

ZESTY LEMON CHIA SEED PUDDING

Take your Simple Chia Seed Pudding and give it a little elegance and zing with the addition of lemon zest.

Calories: **143** Total fat: **7 g** Saturated fat: **0 g** Total carbohydrate: **11 g** Dietary fibre: **3 g** Sugars: **9 g** Protein: **4 g**

1   Follow the instructions for the Simple Chia Seed Pudding (see above), and grate in 1–2 teaspoons of lemon zest with the other ingredients.

Opposite: Simple Chia Seed Pudding topped with mixed berries

🥄 **Try This**

Extra-creamy Chia Seed Pudding
Use DIY Nut Milk (see page 162) for an extra-creamy
decadent pudding.

Yield: 375 g (13 oz)
Serving size: 188 g (6½ oz)

Ingredients

240 ml (8½ fl oz) unsweetened
plant-based milk

40 g (1½ oz) chia seeds

1½ tablespoons maple syrup

½ teaspoon pure vanilla extract

pinch of sea salt

60 g (2½ oz) raspberries (fresh or
frozen, thawed)

1 tablespoon shredded coconut

Yield: 250 g (9 oz)
Serving size: 125 g (4½ oz)

Ingredients

240 ml (8½ fl oz) unsweetened
plant-based milk

40 g (1½ oz) chia seeds

1½ tablespoons maple syrup

½ teaspoon pure vanilla extract

pinch of sea salt

1 tablespoon unsweetened cocoa
powder or raw cacao powder

raw cacao nibs, for topping
(optional)

Yield: 375 g (13 oz)
Serving size: 188 g (6½ oz)

Ingredients

240 ml (8½ fl oz) unsweetened
plant-based milk

40 g (1½ oz) chia seeds

1½ tablespoons maple syrup

½ teaspoon pure vanilla extract

pinch of sea salt

½ teaspoon ground cinnamon

¼ teaspoon ground ginger

pinch of ground nutmeg

60 g (2½ oz) unsweetened pumpkin
purée (fresh or tinned)

COCONUT RASPBERRY CHIA SEED PUDDING

If you're looking for a way to curb those sugar cravings, sweet raspberry and satiating coconut just might do the trick.

Calories: **205** Total fat: **10 g** Saturated fat: **2 g** Total carbohydrate: **15 g**
Dietary fibre: **6 g** Sugars: **10 g** Protein: **6 g**

1 Follow the instructions for the Simple Chia Seed Pudding (see page 68).

2 In a separate bowl, mash the raspberries with a fork or blend in a liquidizer. Mix the chia seed pudding, mashed raspberries and shredded coconut together to serve.

CHOCOLATE CHIA SEED PUDDING

When it is 4 P.M. and you need to make it through to your evening workout, this energizing pudding is the answer.

Calories: **154** Total fat: **7 g** Saturated fat: **0 g** Total carbohydrate: **12 g**
Dietary fibre: **4 g** Sugars: **9 g** Protein: **5 g**

1 Follow the instructions for Simple Chia Seed Pudding (see page 68), adding in the cocoa or raw cacao powder with the other ingredients. Mix well to make sure the powder dissolves. Top with cacao nibs, if desired, for an extra burst of antioxidants and energy.

PUMPKIN SPICE CHIA SEED PUDDING

Pumpkin purée adds fibre and flavour, and the spices contribute a mega-dose of anti-inflammatory properties.

Calories: **185** Total fat: **9 g** Saturated fat: **0 g** Total carbohydrate: **14 g**
Dietary fibre: **4 g** Sugars: **10 g** Protein: **6 g**

1 Follow the instructions for the Simple Chia Seed Pudding (see page 68). Mix in the cinnamon, ginger and nutmeg with the other ingredients, reserving the pumpkin purée. Mix in the pumpkin purée after the chia seed mixture has thickened, just before serving

🥄 **Try This**

Pumpkin Spice Mix
½ teaspoon pumpkin pie spice mix can be used in place of the cinnamon, ginger and nutmeg for the Pumpkin Spice Chia Seed Pudding.

GRAB-AND-GO OVERNIGHT OATS

Yield: 375 g (13 oz)
Serving size: 375 g (13 oz)
Prep time: 5–10 minutes, plus rest overnight
Storage: Up to 3 days in the fridge

Filled with fibre, good-for-you carbs, healthy fats and protein, overnight oats are perfect before an intense workout or a long day. Made the night before, they are the perfect grab-and-go easy morning meal. Eat cold, or heat for a warming start to your day.

BLUEBERRY CASHEW OVERNIGHT OATS

Ingredients
1 tablespoon cashew butter
50 g (2 oz) rolled oats
1 teaspoon maple syrup (or to taste)
120 ml (4 fl oz) unsweetened cashew milk
¼–½ teaspoon grated fresh ginger (or pinch of ground ginger)
pinch of sea salt
110 g (4 fl oz) blueberries, plus a few extra to serve

Blueberries and cashews are a match made in nutrition heaven. The phytonutrient-rich berries give you a powerful punch of nutrients, while the cashews help to keep your blood sugar stable.

Calories: **337** Total fat: **13 g** Saturated fat: **2 g** Total carbohydrate: **52 g** Dietary fibre: **7 g** Sugars: **16 g** Protein: **9 g**

1   In the evening: Mix the cashew butter, oats, maple syrup, cashew milk, grated ginger and salt together. Add the blueberries and stir. Place all the ingredients in a mason jar (or any glass jar) and mix together.

2   In the morning: Stir again and top with extra blueberries and your favourite nutritional boosts (see Toppings panel, page 73). So easy and so good!

BANANA ALMOND CRUNCH OVERNIGHT OATS

Ingredients
½ banana
1 tablespoon almond butter
50 g (2 oz) rolled oats
120 ml (4 fl oz) unsweetened almond milk
½ teaspoon pure vanilla extract
¼ teaspoon ground cinnamon
1 tablespoon buckwheat
1 teaspoon maple syrup (or to taste)
pinch of sea salt

The addition of buckwheat provides a little crunch, and the extra good-for-you carbs work to create a steady and natural rise in blood sugar levels.

Calories: **330** Total fat: **12 g** Saturated fat: **2 g** Total carbohydrate: **47 g** Dietary fibre: **8 g** Sugars: **10 g** Protein: **11 g**

1   Mash the banana and almond butter together before combining all the ingredients in the jar following the same method as the Blueberry Cashew Overnight Oats (see above).

Coconut Raspberry
Overnight Oats,
page 73

Blueberry Cashew
Overnight Oats, page 71

Ingredients

50 g (2 oz) rolled oats

120 ml (4 fl oz) unsweetened coconut milk

1 tablespoon chia seeds

1 tablespoon shredded coconut

1 teaspoon grated lemon zest

1 teaspoon maple syrup (or to taste)

pinch of sea salt

60 g (2½ oz) raspberries

COCONUT RASPBERRY OVERNIGHT OATS

There is no shortage of flavour and nutrition in this nut-free combo with the omega-3-rich chia seeds, coconut, raspberries and lemon zest in the mix.

Calories: **333** Total fat: **13 g** Saturated fat: **7 g** Total carbohydrate: **47 g**
Dietary fibre: **14 g** Sugars: **8 g** Protein: **10 g**

1   Combine all the ingredients together in the jar following the same method as the Blueberry Cashew Overnight Oats (see page 71), adding the raspberries last.

Ingredients

½ ripe pear

50 g (2 oz) rolled oats

120 ml (4 fl oz) unsweetened almond milk

½ teaspoon ground cinnamon

1 tablespoon flax seeds

2 teaspoons almond butter

1 teaspoon maple syrup (or to taste)

pinch of sea salt

PERFECT PEAR OVERNIGHT OATS

Pear provides extra fibre and a creamy texture in this filling and energizing variation.

Calories: **366** Total fat: **15 g** Saturated fat: **2 g** Total carbohydrate: **52 g**
Dietary fibre: **11 g** Sugars: **13 g** Protein: **11 g**

1   Combine all of the ingredients together in the jar, following the same method as the Blueberry Cashew Overnight Oats (see page 71).

Toppings

Why add toppings? Get a nutritional boost, add some texture, create variety and enhance the flavour of smoothies, parfaits and overnight oats with the addition of toppings.

What are toppings? Toppings are fun, colourful, creative and totally customizable. There are no rules. Just think of toppings as an opportunity to switch up a recipe with a different spin each time. Need more protein? Toss on some nuts, seeds or a drizzle of nut butter. Craving crunch with those overnight oats? Chop up apples and almonds to put on top just before eating. The options are limitless.

Note: If you are topping a smoothie or smoothie bowl, make sure that the smoothie is thick enough so that the toppings don't sink.

Topping inspiration:

Shredded coconut

Dried fruit (goji berries, mulberries)

Fresh fruit (mangoes, kiwi, berries, chopped figs, sliced bananas, apples, pears, peaches, pomegranate seeds)

Bee pollen

Seeds (flax seeds, hemp seeds, chia seeds, pumpkin seeds, sunflower seeds)

Nuts (cashews, sliced almonds, crushed walnuts, pecans, macadamia nuts)

Granola

Fresh mint or basil leaves

Drizzles of nut or seed butter

Cinnamon

Cacao powder or cacao nibs

Citrus zest

BAKED OAT CUPS

A hybrid between a bowl of oats and a muffin, these oat cups will give you the right kind of complex carbohydrates that will get you armed and ready to take on even the most challenging workout. Store them in the freezer to have on hand, ready to heat and eat in a flash.

Yield: 12 oat cups

Serving size: 1 oat cup

Prep time: 10 minutes, plus 22–27 minutes baking

Storage: Eat immediately or refrigerate for up to 2 days and reheat, or freeze for up to 1 month

Ingredients

175 g (6 oz) rolled oats

1 teaspoon baking powder

½ teaspoon sea salt

1 teaspoon ground cinnamon

2 tablespoons coconut oil, melted, plus extra for greasing

50 g (2 oz) mashed bananas

240 ml (8½ fl oz) unsweetened almond milk, or any plant-based milk

2 tablespoons maple syrup

75 g (3 oz) chocolate chips

½ banana, sliced, to top

BANANA CHOCOLATE CHIP BAKED OAT CUPS

My husband has officially made this his pre-spin fuel of choice. The banana and chocolate chips combine for an extra energizing and tasty option.

Calories: **136** Total fat: **6 g** Saturated fat: **4 g** Total carbohydrate: **20 g** Dietary fibre: **2 g** Sugars: **8 g** Protein: **3 g**

1 Preheat the oven to 180°C (350°F). Grease a muffin tin with coconut oil.

2 Combine the oats, baking powder, salt and cinnamon in a large bowl.

3 In a separate bowl, combine the coconut oil, mashed banana, almond milk and maple syrup.

4 Add the wet ingredients to the dry ingredients and mix to combine. Add the chocolate chips and stir well.

5 Pour the mixture into the prepared muffin tin, and add sliced banana to the tops of each oat cup before baking.

6 Bake for 22–25 minutes until the cups are a golden brown. Eat immediately or store in the fridge for 2 days or in the freezer for up to 1 month. Reheat before serving.

 Try This

Chocolate Chip Alternative
Use 50 g (2 oz) walnuts instead of (or in addition to) the chocolate for Banana Chocolate Chip Baked Oat Cups.

Lemony Blueberry Baked Oat Cups Variations
Omit the lemon zest for a more traditional blueberry option. You can also replace the egg with apple sauce for a vegan-friendly version.

Ingredients

200 g (7 oz) rolled oats

1 teaspoon baking powder

½ teaspoon sea salt

1 teaspoon ground cinnamon, plus extra to sprinkle

pinch of ground nutmeg

1 teaspoon grated fresh ginger (or ⅓ teaspoon ground)

2 tablespoons ground flax seeds

2 tablespoons coconut oil, melted, plus extra for greasing

110 g (4 oz) unsweetened pumpkin purée (fresh or tinned)

240 ml (8½ fl oz) unsweetened almond milk, or plant-based milk

75 g (3 oz) maple syrup

60 g (2½ oz) pitted Medjool dates, chopped

pumpkin seeds, to top

PUMPKIN DATE BAKED OAT CUPS

Pumpkin is loaded with zinc and vitamin C to help boost your immunity, particularly before the cold and flu season.

Calories: **125** Total fat: **4 g** Saturated fat: **1 g** Total carbohydrate: **21 g**
Dietary fibre: **3 g** Sugars: **7 g** Protein: **3 g**

1   Follow the instructions for the Banana Chocolate Chip Baked Oat Cups (see page 74), combining the ground flax seeds with the other dry ingredients and using pumpkin purée in place of mashed banana. Stir the dates through the mixture just before pouring into the muffin tin. Top with cinnamon and pumpkin seeds. This variation also takes slightly longer to cook (25–27 minutes).

Ingredients

175 g (6 oz) rolled oats

1 teaspoon baking powder

½ teaspoon sea salt

50 g (2 oz) walnuts, chopped, plus extra to top

2 teaspoon grated lemon zest, plus extra to top

2 tablespoons coconut oil, melted, plus extra for greasing

100 g (3½ oz) unsweetened apple sauce (or use 1 egg or 100 g/3½ oz mashed banana)

240 ml (8½ fl oz) unsweetened almond milk, or plant-based milk

1 teaspoon pure vanilla extract

75 g (3 oz) maple syrup

150 g (5 oz) blueberries (frozen work well)

LEMONY BLUEBERRY BAKED OAT CUPS

Lemon and blueberry are a magical pairing that will add an extra dose of vitamin C to your morning routine.

Calories: **133** Total fat: **7 g** Saturated fat: **3 g** Total carbohydrate: **17 g**
Dietary fibre: **2 g** Sugars: **5 g** Protein: **3 g**

1   Follow the instructions for the Banana Chocolate Chip Baked Oat Cups (see page 74), using apple sauce in place of the mashed banana. Make sure not to add the blueberries until the end so that they don't turn the mixture purple. Top with crushed walnuts and lemon zest.

Ingredients

175 g (6 oz) rolled oats

1 teaspoon baking powder

½ teaspoon sea salt

2 tablespoons ground flax seeds

1 teaspoon ground cinnamon

75 g (3 oz) pecans, chopped

2 tablespoons coconut oil, melted, plus extra for greasing

100 g (3½ oz) unsweetened apple sauce

240 ml (8½ fl oz) unsweetened almond milk, or plant-based milk

75 g (3 oz) maple syrup

1 apple, peeled and chopped

APPLE CINNAMON BAKED OAT CUPS

It's like a bowl of cinnamon apple porridge to go! Bonus: cinnamon can help with blood sugar regulation.

Calories: **149** Total fat: **7 g** Saturated fat: **3 g** Total carbohydrate: **21 g**
Dietary fibre: **3 g** Sugars: **8 g** Protein: **3 g**

1   Follow the instructions for the Banana Chocolate Chip Baked Oat Cups (see page 74), combining the ground flax seeds with the other dry ingredients and using the apple sauce in place of the mashed banana. Reserve some chopped apple pieces and pecans to sprinkle on top before baking.

OUT-AND-ABOUT MUFFINS

Yield: 12 muffins
Serving size: 1 muffin
Prep time: 10 minutes,
25–30 minutes baking
Storage: 1 day at room temperature
and 1 month in the freezer

Try these fibre-rich morsels as a great pre-exercise snack or on-the-go breakfast. Each of the recipes has a different nutrition profile, so find the kind that works best for your body and activity level. Some are higher in protein and grain-free, while others are loaded with more complex carbs. They all freeze beautifully and can be ready to eat in a pinch.

Ingredients

1 tablespoon ground flax seeds
3 tablespoons warm water
125 g (4½ oz) almond flour
100 g (3½ oz) quinoa flour
100 g (3½ oz) brown rice flour
1 teaspoon ground cinnamon
1 teaspoon bicarbonate of soda
1 teaspoon baking powder
½ teaspoon sea salt
150 g (5 oz) honey
60 g (2½ oz) coconut oil, softened,
  plus extra for greasing
60 g (2½ oz) apple sauce
120 ml (4 fl oz) unsweetened
  almond milk
1 tablespoon apple cider vinegar
150 g (5 oz) blueberries, frozen
  or fresh

GOOD MORNING BLUEBERRY MUFFINS

Made without any eggs, gluten, dairy or refined flours, these muffins are rich in fibre, making them a nutrient-dense option.

Calories: **214** Total fat: **10 g** Saturated fat: **5 g** Total carbohydrate: **29 g**
Dietary fibre: **3 g** Sugars: **14 g** Protein: **4 g**

1 Preheat the oven to 180°C (350°F). Oil a muffin tin with coconut oil.

2 To make a flax egg, mix the ground flax seeds with the water in a small bowl. Let stand for 10 minutes until a gel-like consistency forms.

3 In a medium bowl, mix almond flour, quinoa flour, brown rice flour, cinnamon, bicarbonate of soda, baking powder and salt. Set aside.

4 In a large bowl, add in honey, coconut oil, the flax egg, apple sauce, almond milk and apple cider vinegar. Mix well. Pour the dry ingredients into the wet ingredients and stir. Add in blueberries and distribute evenly throughout, making sure not to overmix the batter.

5 Fill muffin tins to about three-quarters full and bake for 25–30 minutes, until a skewer inserted in the centre of the muffin comes out clean. Cool before serving.

✎ Try This

Gluten-free Flour Option
Try my versatile DIY gluten-free mixture, or experiment with your own version. For 250 g (9 oz) of flour, use 125 g (4½ oz) brown rice flour, 100 g (3½ oz) sorghum flour and 25 g (1 oz) tapioca flour (or arrowroot).

Ingredients

60 g (2½ oz) coconut flour

1 teaspoon sea salt

¾ teaspoon bicarbonate of soda

5 eggs

125 ml (4½ fl oz) coconut oil, softened, plus extra for oiling

150 g (5 oz) honey

2 tablespoons lemon juice

1 tablespoon grated lemon zest

125 g (4½ oz) raspberries, fresh or frozen (if using frozen, do not thaw)

1½ tablespoons poppy seeds

LEMON POPPY SEED MUFFINS WITH RASPBERRIES

These moist gluten-free and grain-free muffins have a sensational blend of sweet and tart flavour.

Calories: **191** Total fat: **13 g** Saturated fat: **10 g** Total carbohydrate: **17 g** Dietary fibre: **3 g** Sugars: **13 g** Protein: **4 g**

1   Preheat the oven to 180°C (350°F). Lightly oil a muffin tin with coconut oil.

2   In a medium bowl, mix coconut flour, sea salt and bicarbonate of soda. Set aside.

3   In a large bowl, gently whisk the eggs. Add in coconut oil, honey, lemon juice and lemon zest, and mix.

4   Pour the dry ingredients into the wet ingredients and stir. Add in raspberries and poppy seeds and distribute evenly throughout, making sure not to overmix the batter.

5   Fill muffin tins about three-quarters full and bake for 22–25 minutes, until a skewer inserted in the centre of the muffin comes out clean. Cool before serving.

 Cook's Note

Storing Muffins
The Chai Spiced Carrot Muffins (see page 79) and Lemon Poppy Seed Muffins should be stored in the freezer and reheated before eating.

Below: Lemon Poppy Seed Muffins with Raspberries

Ingredients

125 g (4½ oz) millet flour

125 g (4½ oz) brown rice flour

25 g (1 oz) tapioca flour

1 teaspoon bicarbonate of soda

1 teaspoon baking powder

½ teaspoon sea salt

2 eggs, whisked

60 g (2½ oz) coconut oil, softened, plus extra for greasing

60 g (2½ oz) honey

1 tablespoon apple cider vinegar

1 teaspoon pure vanilla extract

240 ml (8½ fl oz) unsweetened almond milk

MILLET MUFFINS

A not-too-sweet muffin that tastes just as good with chia jam (see page 106) or accompanying a savoury blended soup (see page 46).

Calories: **177** Total fat: **6 g** Saturated fat: **5 g** Total carbohydrate: **28 g**
Dietary fibre: **2 g** Sugars: **8 g** Protein: **3 g**

1 Preheat the oven to 180°C (350°F). Lightly oil a muffin tin with coconut oil.

2 In a medium bowl, mix millet flour, brown rice flour, tapioca flour, bicarbonate of soda, baking powder and salt. Set aside.

3 In a large bowl, combine the whisked eggs, coconut oil, honey, apple cider vinegar and vanilla extract. Whisk. Pour in almond milk and mix well.

4 Add the dry ingredients to the wet ingredients and stir to incorporate evenly.

5 Fill muffin tins about three-quarters full. Bake for 20–22 minutes, until the muffins are golden brown and a skewer inserted in the centre comes out clean. Cool before serving.

Ingredients

175 g (6 oz) almond flour

60 g (2½ oz) coconut flour

1 teaspoon ground cinnamon

25 g (1 oz) arrowroot or tapioca flour

1 teaspoon bicarbonate of soda

½ teaspoon sea salt

2 eggs

55 ml (2 fl oz) maple syrup

110 g (4 oz) coconut oil, melted, plus extra for greasing

1 teaspoon pure vanilla extract

3 mashed bananas

75 g (3 oz) chocolate chips

GRAIN-FREE GOOEY BANANA CHOCOLATE CHIP MUFFINS

My son Noah created these delicious muffins containing the perfect combination of protein, fibre and healthy fat. A great choice for blood sugar stabilization.

Calories: **284** Total fat: **20 g** Saturated fat: **12 g** Total carbohydrate: **24 g**
Dietary fibre: **5 g** Sugars: **12 g** Protein: **5 g**

1 Preheat the oven to 180°C (350°F) and lightly oil a muffin tin with coconut oil.

2 Mix the almond flour, coconut flour, cinnamon, arrowroot, bicarbonate of soda and salt in a medium bowl and set aside.

3 Whisk the eggs in a large bowl, then add the maple syrup, coconut oil and vanilla extract. Mix well. Add the mashed banana and mix again.

4 Pour the dry ingredients into the wet ingredients and stir. Add the chocolate chips and distribute evenly throughout.

5 Fill the muffin tins about three-quarters full and bake for 25–30 minutes, until a skewer inserted in the centre of the muffin comes out clean. Cool before serving.

 Cook's Note

Bananas for Gooey Banana Chocolate Chip Muffins
Avoid using overripe bananas, as it alters the muffins' flavour.

Ingredients

60 g (2½ oz) coconut flour

1 teaspoon ground cardamom

2 teaspoons ground cinnamon

½ teaspoon ground ginger

¼ teaspoon ground cloves

¼ teaspoon ground nutmeg

1 teaspoon sea salt

½ teaspoon bicarbonate of soda

5 eggs

110 g (4 oz) coconut oil, softened, plus extra for greasing

150 g (5 oz) honey

1 teaspoon pure vanilla extract

125 g (4½ oz) shredded carrots

60 g (2½ oz) chopped walnuts

CHAI SPICED CARROT MUFFINS

Exploding with flavour and anti-inflammatory spices, plus plenty of fibre, these muffins are satisfying, wholesome and sweet.

Calories: **212** Total fat: **15 g** Saturated fat: **10 g** Total carbohydrate: **17 g**
Dietary fibre: **3 g** Sugars: **13 g** Protein: **4 g**

1   Preheat the oven to 180°C (350°F). Lightly oil a muffin tin with coconut oil.

2   In a medium bowl, mix flour, cardamom, cinnamon, ginger, cloves, nutmeg, sea salt and bicarbonate of soda. Set aside.

3   In a large bowl, gently whisk the eggs. Add in coconut oil, honey and vanilla extract, and mix.

4   Pour the dry ingredients into the wet ingredients and stir. Add in shredded carrots and walnuts, and mix gently until well combined.

5   Fill muffin tins about three-quarters full and bake for 20–22 minutes, until a skewer inserted in the centre of the muffin comes out clean. Cool before serving.

Ingredients

100 g (3½ oz) almond flour

125 g (4½ oz) gluten-free flour (see Try This note, page 76)

1 teaspoon baking powder

1 teaspoon ground cinnamon

½ teaspoon ground cardamom

½ teaspoon sea salt

2 eggs

75 g (3 fl oz) maple syrup

60 g (2½ oz) coconut oil, softened, plus extra for greasing

40 g (1½ oz) shredded coconut

125 g (4½ oz) grated carrots

125 g (4½ oz) grated apples

APPLE SPICED MUFFINS

How can you go wrong with coconut, apple and carrots all in one muffin?

Calories: **178** Total fat: **10 g** Saturated fat: **6 g** Total carbohydrate: **20 g**
Dietary fibre: **2 g** Sugars: **5 g** Protein: **4 g**

1   Preheat the oven to 180°C (350°F). Lightly oil a muffin tin with coconut oil.

2   In a medium bowl, mix almond flour, gluten-free flour, baking powder, cinnamon, cardamom and sea salt. Set aside.

3   In a large bowl, whisk eggs and add in maple syrup and coconut oil. Mix well.

4   Pour the dry ingredients into the wet ingredients and stir. Add in shredded coconut, grated carrots and grated apple and mix well.

5   Fill muffin tins about three-quarters full and bake for 25–30 minutes, until a skewer inserted in the centre of the muffin comes out clean. Cool before serving.

FRITTATA CUPS

Yield: 12 muffins
Serving size: 1 muffin
Prep time: 5–10 minutes, 25 minutes baking time
Storage: Up to 3 days in the fridge – reheat before eating

When your body is telling you that it needs protein, this frittata cup is for you. Make a tray ahead of time and then heat up your 'muffin' whenever you need to balance your blood sugar. Top with chopped avocado, hot sauce and/or salsa for a satisfying post-workout breakfast or between-meals snack.

Ingredients
olive oil or coconut oil, for greasing
12 large eggs
splash of water
20 g (¾ oz) spinach, thinly sliced
25 g (1 oz) diced onion
60 g (2½ oz) seeds removed and diced red peppers
½ teaspoon sea salt
¼ teaspoon freshly ground black pepper

COLOURFUL MIXED VEGGIE FRITTATA CUPS

Eating a variety of colourful produce is a great way to improve your overall nutrition. Try using spinach, red pepper and onion, and then vary it with other hues added to the mix.

Calories: **68** Total fat: **4 g** Saturated fat: **1 g** Total carbohydrate: **1 g**
Dietary fibre: **0 g** Sugars: **1 g** Protein: **6 g**

1 Preheat the oven to 180°C (350°F) and lightly oil a muffin pan with olive oil or coconut oil.

2 Whisk the eggs in a medium-large bowl and add a splash of water. Fold in the vegetables and mix well. Season with salt and pepper.

3 Fill the muffin tins about three-quarters full and bake for 20–25 minutes, removing from the oven once the eggs are set in the middle and lightly golden on top.

Ingredients
olive oil or coconut oil, for greasing
12 large eggs
splash of water
75 g (3 oz) tomatoes, diced
10 g (½ oz) fresh basil, thinly sliced
1 garlic clove, minced (optional)
½ teaspoon sea salt
¼ teaspoon freshly ground black pepper

TOMATO BASIL FRITTATA CUPS

Enjoy the tastes of Italy with fresh tomatoes, garlic and basil.

Calories: **67** Total fat: **4 g** Saturated fat: **1 g** Total carbohydrate: **1 g**
Dietary fibre: **0 g** Sugars: **1 g** Protein: **6 g**

1 Follow the instructions for the Colourful Mixed Veggie Frittata Cups (see above), adding the herb flavourings with the tomatoes.

Opposite: Colourful Mixed Veggie Frittata Cups

🥄 **Cook's Note**

Oil the Muffin Tin
Make sure to oil the muffin tin well so the frittatas can be easily removed once cooked.

Ingredients

olive oil or coconut oil, for greasing

12 large eggs

splash of water

40 g (1½ oz) kale, thinly sliced

25 g (1 oz) grated courgettes

2 garlic cloves, minced

½ teaspoon sea salt

¼ teaspoon freshly ground black pepper

Ingredients

olive oil or coconut oil, for greasing

12 large eggs

splash of water

75 g (3 oz) tomatoes, diced

25 g (1 oz) thinly sliced spring onions

10 g (½ oz) fresh coriander, chopped

½–1 jalapeño pepper (optional)

½ teaspoon sea salt

¼ teaspoon freshly ground black pepper

GO GREEN FRITTATA CUPS

An easy way to sneak in some more greens! Mix and match your favourite leafy greens, or stick with the kale – my favourite.

Calories: **67** Total fat: **4 g** Saturated fat: **1 g** Total carbohydrate: **1 g**
Dietary fibre: **0 g** Sugars: **0 g** Protein: **6 g**

1 Follow the instructions for the Colourful Mixed Veggie Frittata Cups (see page 80), adding the garlic with the vegetables.

SOUTHWESTERN FRITTATA CUPS

The most flavourful frittata of the bunch works beautifully when topped with chopped avocado or guacamole (see page 99), black beans and salsa for a more substantial meal or snack.

Calories: **68** Total fat: **4 g** Saturated fat: **1 g** Total carbohydrate: **1 g**
Dietary fibre: **0 g** Sugars: **1 g** Protein: **6 g**

1 Follow the instructions for the Colourful Mixed Veggie Frittata Cups (see page 80), adding the herb flavourings with the vegetables. Serve topped with salsa, avocado and black beans.

Below: Serve the Southwestern Frittata Cups with Green on Green Guacamole, page 100.

GRANOLAS AND TRAIL MIXES

When you're out on a long hike or bike ride, you'll need one of the portable recipes from this chapter to power you through. You can adapt granolas and trail mixes to suit your individual energy needs and even combine them with other recipes. Try granola as a topping on a Smoothie Bowl (see page 38), sprinkle the trail mix on the Banana Ice Cream to add crunch (see page 146) or top your salad with the Supercharged Seed Mix (see page 90) for a nutritional boost.

Almond Butter and Chocolate
Granola, page 87

GRANOLAS

Yield: See each recipe

Serving size: See each recipe

Prep time: 10–15 minutes, plus 25–35 minutes cooking

Storage: Up to 3 weeks at room temperature

Note: Buckwheat Crunchy Granola and Sunflower Butter stores up to 2 weeks. Coated granolas (page 87) keep for 5 days at room temperature; freeze for longer storage.

Homemade granola makes a quick breakfast, snack or afternoon pick-me-up. These versions are filled with omega-rich (healthy) fats and a lot less sugar than the commercial packaged varieties. Mix and match with different combinations and flavours to create a unique batch each time. The recipes here include energizing granolas perfect for starting the day (see pages 85–86) and coated granolas to provide you with slow-release, sustaining energy (see page 87).

Yield: 1 kg (2¼ lb)
Serving size: 40 g (1½ oz)

Ingredients

160 ml (5½ fl oz) maple syrup

1 teaspoon pure vanilla extract

2 tablespoons coconut oil, melted

275 g (10 oz) rolled oats

75 g (3 oz) shredded coconut

2 teaspoons ground cinnamon

1 teaspoon sea salt

175 g (6 oz) almonds (or walnuts, or half of each)

75 g (3 oz) pumpkin seeds

75 g (3 oz) sunflower seeds

60 g (1½ oz) goji berries (optional)

VANILLA MAPLE CRUNCH GRANOLA

This delicious granola is perfect any time you need an energizing snack that will keep your blood sugar balanced. Serve with nut milk, layered in parfaits or enjoy on its own.

Calories: **149** Total fat: **9 g** Saturated fat: **5 g** Total carbohydrate: **14 g**
Dietary fibre: **2 g** Sugars: **6 g** Protein: **4 g**

1 Preheat the oven to 170°C (325°F) and line 2 baking sheets with baking paper.

2 Place the maple syrup, vanilla extract and coconut oil in a small bowl. Place the oats, coconut, cinnamon, salt, nuts and seeds in a large bowl. Add the wet ingredients to the dry ingredients and mix with a spoon to coat evenly.

3 Spread the mixture onto the baking sheets. Bake for 35 minutes, stirring after 20 minutes. For clumpier granola, lightly stir only once with a wooden spoon.

4 Once evenly browned, remove from the oven and let cool completely. Add the goji berries, if using, and mix. Enjoy!

Yield: 700 g (1½ lb)
Serving size: 25 g (1 oz)

Ingredients

2 ripe mashed bananas

3 tablespoons maple syrup (honey works too)

2 tablespoons coconut oil, melted

½ teaspoon pure vanilla extract

240 g (8½ oz) buckwheat

75 g (3 oz) coconut flakes

100 g (3½ oz) walnuts, coarsely chopped

75 g (3 oz) pumpkin seeds

1 teaspoon ground cinnamon

½ teaspoon sea salt

BUCKWHEAT CRUNCHY GRANOLA

Buckwheat makes a wonderful crunchy base in this oat-free granola. This recipe uses two ripe bananas and only a few tablespoons of maple syrup to naturally sweeten this lower-sugar granola.

Calories: **161** Total fat: **9 g** Saturated fat: **5 g** Total carbohydrate: **19 g**
Dietary fibre: **3 g** Sugars: **4 g** Protein: **4 g**

1 Follow the instructions for Vanilla Maple Crunch Granola (see above), but bake for 25–30 minutes, lightly stirring after 15 minutes.

 Cook's Notes

Keep an Eye on the Oven
Ovens may vary, so check the granola often while cooking, as it can burn easily.

Buckwheat
This naturally gluten-free whole food is actually a fruit seed and not a grain, despite its name.

Mashed Bananas for Buckwheat Crunchy Granola
It is best to mash your bananas for the Buckwheat Crunchy Granola with a fork. When adding to the dry mixture, be sure to coat well.

Opposite: Vanilla Maple Crunch Granola

Yield: 900 g (2 lb)
Serving size: 40 g (1½ oz)

Ingredients

160 ml (5½ oz) maple syrup

1 teaspoon pure vanilla extract

2 tablespoons coconut oil, melted

275 g (10 oz) rolled oats

75 g (3 oz) coconut flakes

2 teaspoons ground cinnamon

1 teaspoon sea salt

150 g (5 oz) pumpkin seeds

150 g (5 oz) sunflower seeds

150 g (5 oz) hemp seeds

60 g (2½ oz) chopped dried apricots
(optional)

Yield: 575 g (1¼ lb)
Serving size: 25 g (1 oz)

Ingredients

75 ml (3 fl oz) maple syrup

1 teaspoon pure vanilla extract

3 tablespoons olive oil

40 g (1½ oz) quinoa

175 g (6 oz) rolled oats

3 tablespoons ground flax seeds

100 g (3½ oz) pecans, chopped

75 g (3 oz) coconut flakes

½ teaspoon sea salt

1 tablespoon grated orange zest

60 g (2½ oz) dried cranberries

THREE-SEED GRANOLA

Omit the nuts and add in seeds for a big dose of micronutrients – vitamins and minerals galore.

Calories: **149** Total fat: **9 g** Saturated fat: **4 g** Total carbohydrate: **15 g**
Dietary fibre: **2 g** Sugars: **6 g** Protein: **5 g**

1 Follow the instructions for the Vanilla Maple Crunch Granola (see page 85), adding the dried fruit after baking, if using.

CRANBERRY ORANGE QUINOA GRANOLA

Quinoa adds crunch, orange zest and cranberries burst with vitamin C, and flax seeds and pecans pack in healthy unsaturated fat.

Calories: **157** Total fat: **9 g** Saturated fat: **3 g** Total carbohydrate: **17 g**
Dietary fibre: **3 g** Sugars: **4 g** Protein: **3 g**

1 Follow the instructions for the Vanilla Maple Crunch Granola (see page 85), but bake for 25–30 minutes (lightly stirring after 15 minutes) and add the dried cranberries after baking.

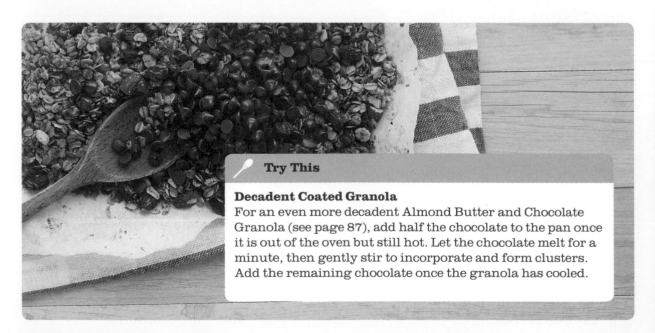

🥄 **Try This**

Decadent Coated Granola
For an even more decadent Almond Butter and Chocolate Granola (see page 87), add half the chocolate to the pan once it is out of the oven but still hot. Let the chocolate melt for a minute, then gently stir to incorporate and form clusters. Add the remaining chocolate once the granola has cooled.

Yield: 700 g (1½ lb)
Serving size: 40 g (1½ oz)

Ingredients

50 g (2 oz) almond butter

50 g (2 oz) coconut oil

60 ml (2½ fl oz) maple syrup

1 teaspoon pure vanilla extract

275 g (10 oz) rolled oats

175 g (6 oz) almonds, coarsely chopped

1 teaspoon sea salt

125 g (4½ oz) chocolate chunks or chocolate chips (good quality and dark)

ALMOND BUTTER AND CHOCOLATE GRANOLA

I created this smoother granola for my son Daniel, who loves the flavour (and nutrition) of nuts but not the texture.

Calories: **139** Total fat: **8 g** Saturated fat: **4 g** Total carbohydrate: **15 g** Dietary fibre: **2 g** Sugars: **6 g** Protein: **3 g**

1 Preheat the oven to 170°C (325°F) and line a baking sheet with baking paper.

2 Gently heat the almond butter and coconut oil in a small saucepan. Remove from the heat when the mixture has liquefied. Once slightly cooled, add the maple syrup and vanilla extract. Mix all the dry ingredients, except for the chocolate, in a large bowl. Add the wet ingredients to the dry mixture and stir until evenly coated.

3 Spread in a single layer on the baking sheet and bake for 25–30 minutes, checking every 10 minutes. Remove from the oven once slightly browned. Once cooled, add the chocolate chunks.

Yield: 700 g (1½ lb)
Serving size: 25 g (1 oz)

Ingredients

60 g (2½ oz) sunflower seed butter

60 g (2½ oz) coconut oil

60 ml (2½ fl oz) maple syrup

1 tablespoon molasses (optional)

1 teaspoon pure vanilla extract

275 g (10 oz) rolled oats

150 g (5 oz) sunflower seeds

1 tablespoon grated fresh ginger (or 1 teaspoon ground)

2 teaspoons ground cinnamon

¼ teaspoon ground nutmeg

¼ teaspoon allspice

1 teaspoon sea salt

125 g (4½ oz) dried figs, chopped

SUNFLOWER BUTTER AND FIG SPICED GRANOLA

Seeds boost your intake of magnesium, a mineral that is necessary for healthy bones and energy production. Plus, this nut-free variation is my favourite!

Calories: **127** Total fat: **7 g** Saturated fat: **3 g** Total carbohydrate: **15 g** Dietary fibre: **2 g** Sugars: **5 g** Protein: **3 g**

1 Follow the instructions for the Almond Butter and Chocolate Granola (see above), adding the dried figs once cooled.

Yield: 700 g (1½ lb)
Serving size: 25 g (1 oz)

Ingredients

60 g (2½ oz) cashew butter

60 g (2½ oz) coconut oil

60 ml (2½ fl oz) maple syrup

1 teaspoon pure vanilla extract

275 g (10 oz) rolled oats

1 teaspoon sea salt

175 g (6 oz) cashews, coarsely chopped

75 g (3 oz) coconut flakes

60 g (2½ oz) goji berries

CASHEW BUTTER, COCONUT AND GOJI BERRY GRANOLA

Goji berries aren't considered a superfood for no reason. They are extremely high in vitamin C and also low in natural sugar.

Calories: **144** Total fat: **8 g** Saturated fat: **4 g** Total carbohydrate: **15 g** Dietary fibre: **2 g** Sugars: **3 g** Protein: **4 g**

1 Follow the instructions for the Almond Butter and Chocolate Granola (see above), adding the goji berries once cooled.

TRAIL MIXES

Yield: 600 g (1¼ lb)
Serving size: 40 g (1½ oz)
Prep time: 5–10 minutes
Storage: Up to 10 days at room temperature in an airtight container unless otherwise noted – if using roasted chickpeas, eat the same day

Trail mix is an easy on-the-go snack that helps stabilize blood sugar in-between meals. Pack up individual servings to throw into your bag; you never know when you'll need a handy snack to energize you. Use these recipes as inspiration to create your own using roasted nuts, granola or even chickpeas, then mix and match away!

Superfood Trail Mix, page 89

On-the-Go Super Seeds, page 90

Tropical Trail Mix, page 89

SUPERFOOD TRAIL MIX

Ingredients

75 g (3 oz) sunflower seeds

75 g (3 oz) walnuts

175 g (6 oz) cashews (or almonds)

60 g (2½ oz) goji berries

75 g (3 oz) mulberries

40 g (1½ oz) coconut flakes

25 g (1 oz) cacao nibs

The superfoods in this completely raw version of trail mix are loaded with antioxidants and anti-inflammatory properties.

Calories: **147** Total fat: **10 g** Saturated fat: **2 g** Total carbohydrate: **11 g**
Dietary fibre: **2 g** Sugars: **4 g** Protein: **5 g**

1 Mix all the ingredients together in a bowl. Store in mason jars or an airtight container.

TROPICAL TRAIL MIX

Ingredients

200 g (7 oz) Vanilla Orange Cashews (see page 111) (or use Spicy Coconut Curry Cashews, see page 110, for a sweet and spicy trail mix)

150 g (5 oz) macadamia nuts, roughly chopped

75 g (3 oz) pumpkin seeds

75 g (3 oz) dried mango, roughly chopped

75 g (3 oz) dried pineapple, cut into bite-sized chunks

40 g (1½ oz) coconut flakes

A fantastic portable snack, you're going to want to keep this trail mix close by at all times. It tastes divine sprinkled on top of the Mango Banana Ice Cream (see page 148).

Calories: **157** Total fat: **12 g** Saturated fat: **3 g** Total carbohydrate: **12 g**
Dietary fibre: **1 g** Sugars: **7 g** Protein: **3 g**

1 Mix all the ingredients together in a large bowl. Store in an airtight container and consume within 7 days.

SEEDED TRAIL MIX

Ingredients

75 g (3 oz) pumpkin seeds

75 g (3 oz) sunflower seeds

110 g (4 oz) Three-Seed Granola (see page 86)

100 g (3½ oz) dried blueberries

60 g (2½ oz) dried apricots, chopped

Go nut-free by combining micronutrient-rich seeds with flavourful granola. The dried apricots add just enough sweetness, plus vitamin C, potassium and fibre for a winning combo.

Calories: **130** Total fat: **6 g** Saturated fat: **2 g** Total carbohydrate: **15 g**
Dietary fibre: **3 g** Sugars: **10 g** Protein: **3 g**

1 Mix all the ingredients together in a bowl. Store in mason jars or an airtight container.

🥄 Try This

Seeded Trail Mix Toasted Variation
Try toasting the pumpkin and sunflower seeds in a dry frying pan for 4–5 minutes. Season with sea salt to taste. Cool before mixing with the other ingredients.

On-the-Go Super Seeds Variation
For a superfood version of the On-the-Go Super Seeds (see page 90), add 2 tablespoons of shredded coconut with the hemp seeds and flax seeds. Mix in 1–2 tablespoons cacao nibs and 2 tablespoons goji berries once cooled.

Ingredients

275 g (10 oz) Spicy Mixed Nuts
(see page 111)

40 g (1½ oz) flaked coconut

60 g (2½ oz) dried cherries

60 g (2½ oz) golden raisins

60 g (2½ oz) dark chocolate chunks
(or use Cacao-Dusted Almonds, see
page 112)

SWEET AND SPICY TRAIL MIX

Enjoy the heat of the cayenne pepper and chilli powder layered with the sweetness of the cherries and the chunks of chocolate.

Calories: **185** Total fat: **14 g** Saturated fat: **4 g** Total carbohydrate: **15 g**
Dietary fibre: **3 g** Sugars: **10 g** Protein: **3 g**

1   Mix all the ingredients together in a bowl. Add the chocolate and stir through. Store in an airtight container.

Ingredients

200 g (7 oz) Roasted Chickpeas (Sea
Salt, Paprika, Ground Cumin and
Cinnamon Chickpeas, see page 108)

175 g (6 oz) roasted almonds

100 g (3½ oz) dried cherries

125 g (4½ oz) golden raisins

SWEET AND SAVOURY TRAIL MIX

Boost your plant-based protein and fibre by adding roasted chickpeas into the mix.

Calories: **115** Total fat: **5 g** Saturated fat: **0 g** Total carbohydrate: **15 g**
Dietary fibre: **3 g** Sugars: **9 g** Protein: **3 g**

1   Mix all the ingredients together in a bowl. Best eaten immediately, as the chickpeas lose crispiness the next day.

Yield: 175 g (6 oz)
Serving size: 1 tablespoon
Prep time: 10 minutes
Storage: Up to 3 weeks in an
airtight container

SUPERCHARGED SEED MIX

For those times when you're travelling or out and about and you need a little extra boost, carry a small amount of this portable seed mixture to enhance the nutritional profile of your meal or snack.

Ingredients

75 g (3 oz) raw sunflower seeds

75 g (3 oz) pumpkin seeds, shelled

2 tablespoons hemp seeds

2 tablespoons flax seeds

¼ teaspoon sea salt

ON-THE-GO SUPER SEEDS

With a few additions, this recipe can be made either sweet or savoury – customize it depending on how you will be using your mix.

Calories: **51** Total fat: **4 g** Saturated fat: **1 g** Total carbohydrate: **1 g**
Dietary fibre: **1 g** Sugars: **0 g** Protein: **2 g**

1   Heat a frying pan over medium heat. Once warm, add the sunflower and pumpkin seeds. Dry roast by shaking back and forth for 3–4 minutes until slightly browned. Add in the hemp seeds and flax seeds for 30–45 seconds over low heat. Sprinkle with sea salt while still hot and mix well. Remove from the heat and cool before storing in a glass container or jar.

QUICK BITES

When you hit that afternoon slump or need something to grab before your evening exercise class, these recipes are for you. Delicious savoury dips, stuffed dates, roasted chickpeas and spiced nuts are all packed full of nutrients to keep you going. Mix and match with other recipes to create a more substantial whole food snack or light meal.

Seeded Crackers, page 93;
Garlicky Hummus, page 95

WHOLE FOOD CRACKERS

Yield: 30 crackers

Serving size: 3 crackers

Prep time: 10 minutes, plus 25 minutes baking

Storage: Up to 4 days at room temperature in an airtight container

Note: Almond Pulp Cracker recipe makes slightly less than the other recipes; yield is 20 crackers

Look at the shelves in any grocery store, and it's pretty obvious that crackers are a big business. Unfortunately, most ready-made versions are filled with stripped-down flours and other processed ingredients. These homemade versions are loaded with seeds, whole-grain and grain-free flours and fresh herbs and spices. Pair them with soups, cashew cream cheese or any of the dips for a satisfying and crunchy light meal or snack.

🍳 Cook's Note

Flax/Chia Egg

For people who follow a vegan diet or have a sensitivity or allergy to eggs, the flax/chia egg can be used as an egg substitute in many other recipes that call for eggs. Plus, it also adds a dose of omega-3 to a dish.

The Way It Works Use chia seeds or ground flax seeds. Combine 1 tablespoon of chia seeds or ground flax seeds with 3 tablespoons of warm water in a small bowl. Stir well and then let the mixture sit for 10 minutes. It will form into a gel-like consistency that can be used as an egg substitute.

Ingredients

1 tablespoon chia seeds
3 tablespoons water
175 g (6 oz) almond flour
60 g (2½ oz) quinoa flour
1 tablespoon olive oil
½ teaspoon sea salt
1 tablespoon hemp seeds
1 tablespoon sunflower seeds
1 tablespoon pumpkin seeds
2 tablespoons nutritional yeast
3 tablespoons fresh chives
2 teaspoons honey
55 ml (2 fl oz) water, as needed
1 tablespoon sesame seeds

SEEDED CRACKERS

Seeds may be tiny, but they are nutritionally mighty. Take your crackers to a whole new level with four different seeds added to the mix.

Calories: **148** Total fat: **10 g** Saturated fat: **1 g** Total carbohydrate: **8 g**
Dietary fibre: **4 g** Sugars: **1 g** Protein: **6 g**

1   Preheat the oven to 170°C (325°F) and line a large rimmed baking sheet with baking paper.

2   Mix the chia seeds with the water in a small bowl. Allow to stand for 10 minutes until a gel-like consistency forms.

3   Place both flours, the olive oil and salt in a food processor and pulse 10 times. Add all the seeds (except the sesame seeds), the chia egg, nutritional yeast, chives and honey, and pulse until combined, leaving a little texture.

4   Gradually add in the water and process until the dough comes together and forms a ball on the side of the bowl. The mixture should resemble a thick dough.

5   Place the dough on the lined baking sheet and place a piece of baking paper on top. Use a rolling pin to flatten the dough and make it paper-thin. Remove the paper and sprinkle the sesame seeds on top.

6   Use a knife to score the crackers in rows of 5 across and rows of 6 down (30 crackers total). Bake for 22–25 minutes, or until the edges become firm and the crackers are golden brown.

7   Remove the tray from the oven and allow to cool and crisp up before slicing into squares or breaking into pieces.

Ingredients

1 tablespoon chia seeds
3 tablespoons water
110 g (4 oz) almond flour
60 g (2½ oz) chickpea flour
60 g (2½ oz) brown rice flour
1 tablespoon olive oil
1 teaspoon sea salt
2 tablespoons nutritional yeast
40 g (1½ oz) sesame seeds
1 tablespoon pumpkin seeds
1 teaspoon ground cumin
2 tablespoons lemon juice
½ teaspoon garlic granules
10 g (½ oz) fresh parsley
55 ml (2 fl oz) water, as needed

FALAFEL CRACKERS

My boys love this Mediterranean-inspired cracker, which resembles the taste of a freshly made falafel.

Calories: **155** Total fat: **9 g** Saturated fat: **1 g** Total carbohydrate: **15 g**
Dietary fibre: **4 g** Sugars: **1 g** Protein: **6 g**

1   Follow the instructions for the Seeded Crackers (see above), reserving the parsley and 1 tablespoon of the sesame seeds until the last part of processing – add the parsley at the end, and pulse about 10–12 times to incorporate, leaving some texture. Sprinkle the sesame seeds on the crackers before scoring and placing in the oven to bake.

Opposite: Falafel Crackers

Ingredients

1 tablespoon ground flax seeds

3 tablespoons water

110 g (4 oz) quinoa flour

110 g (4 oz) brown rice flour

2 tablespoons coconut oil

1 teaspoon sea salt

2 tablespoons nutritional yeast

1 tablespoon hemp seeds

2 tablespoon pumpkin seeds

1 teaspoon granulated garlic

½ teaspoon turmeric powder

¼ teaspoon freshly ground black pepper

½ teaspoon chilli flakes (or more for extra spice)

55 ml (2 fl oz) water, as needed

Yield: 20 crackers

Ingredients

1 tablespoon ground flax seeds

3 tablespoons water

200 g (7 oz) almond pulp – this is the amount leftover from 1 batch of almond milk (see page 162)

2 tablespoons olive oil

½ teaspoon sea salt

½ teaspoon dried basil

½ teaspoon dried oregano

¼ teaspoon crushed chilli flakes (or more for a spicy kick)

2 tablespoons chopped fresh parsley

SPICED SEEDED CRACKERS

The turmeric, pepper and chilli flakes give a warming and spicy flair to these nutrient-filled seeded crackers.

Calories: **158** Total fat: **6 g** Saturated fat: **3 g** Total carbohydrate: **23 g**
Dietary fibre: **3 g** Sugars: **0 g** Protein: **5 g**

1   Follow the instructions for the Seeded Crackers (see page 93), making a flax egg at step 2 and reserving the spices (turmeric, garlic and peppers) until the last part of processing – add them at the end, and pulse about 10–12 times to incorporate into the mixture.

ALMOND PULP CRACKERS

Transform the fibre-loaded leftover pulp from your almond milk (see page 162) into grain-free crackers. Substitute different spices to make your own flavours.

Calories: **30** Total fat: **3 g** Saturated fat: **0 g** Total carbohydrate: **1 g**
Dietary fibre: **1 g** Sugars: **0 g** Protein: **1 g**

1   Preheat the oven to 180°C (350°F) and line a large rimmed baking sheet with baking paper.

2   In a small bowl, mix the ground flax seed with the water and let stand for 10 minutes until a gel-like consistency forms.

3   Use your hands to squeeze the almond pulp to remove any excess water and then place in a large mixing bowl. Add the olive oil, salt and flax egg and mix well. Add the basil, oregano, crushed chilli flakes and fresh parsley, and combine. The mixture will be crumbly at first but will eventually form a ball of dough – using your hands works well.

4   Put the dough on the lined baking sheet and place a second piece of baking paper on top. Use a roller to flatten the dough until it is very thin. Remove the second sheet of baking paper. The pulp cracker recipe makes less than the others, so the mixture won't fill the baking sheet completely. Square the edges to neaten. Use a knife to score the crackers in rows of 5 across and rows of 4 down (20 crackers total).

5   Bake for 25–28 minutes, or until the edges become firm and the crackers are golden brown. Remove from the oven and allow to cool before breaking into individual crackers.

HUMMUS

Yield: See each recipe
Serving size: 60 g (2½ oz)
Prep time: 10 minutes (plus 20 minutes roasting time for the carrot hummus)
Storage: Up to 4 days in the fridge in an airtight container

Open up my fridge and you will likely find a fresh batch of hummus. It's a tasty way to get a supply of plant-based protein and healthy fat that happens to be nut-free too. Slice up some carrots, celery, peppers or jicama for dipping, and toss in a handful of crackers (see page 92) for a satisfying mid-afternoon snack.

Yield: 425 g (15 oz)

Ingredients

200 g (7 oz) chickpeas (1 x 425-g/15-oz tin), rinsed and drained

1 large garlic clove, minced

2 tablespoons lemon juice

60 g (2½ oz) tahini

2 tablespoons olive oil

½ teaspoon ground cumin

1 teaspoon grated lemon zest

½ teaspoon sea salt (or to taste)

2–4 tablespoons water

chopped fresh flat-leaf parsley, paprika and a drizzle of olive oil, to top

GARLICKY HUMMUS

A simply delicious hummus that is easy to whip up any time you need a savoury bite. Great with sliced veggies.

Calories: **161** Total fat: **11 g** Saturated fat: **2 g** Total carbohydrate: **10 g** Dietary fibre: **3 g** Sugars: **0 g** Protein: **5 g**

1 Place the chickpeas, garlic, lemon juice, tahini and olive oil in a food processor and process until combined. Add the cumin, lemon zest and salt, and process again.

2 With the motor running, slowly drizzle in the water until the desired consistency is reached. Process until completely smooth and creamy, scraping down the sides of the container if necessary. Adjust the seasonings to taste.

3 Transfer to a bowl and serve topped with chopped flat-leaf parsley, a sprinkle of paprika and a drizzle of olive oil.

Yield: 500 g (1 lb 2 oz)

Ingredients

200 g (7 oz) cooked chickpeas (1 x 425-g/15-oz tin), rinsed and drained

1 garlic clove, minced

60 g (2½ oz) tahini

1 avocado, peeled and pitted

2–3 tablespoons lime juice

½–1 jalapeño pepper, seeds removed

½ teaspoon ground cumin

1 teaspoon grated lime zest

½ teaspoon sea salt

2–3 tablespoons water

2 tablespoons fresh coriander, plus extra to top

crushed chilli flakes, to top (optional)

GUACAMOLE HUMMUS

Avocado and hummus unite for a real nutritional treat. The healthy fat will give you more staying power to sustain you in-between lunch, meetings, Pilates and dinner.

Calories: **157** Total fat: **11 g** Saturated fat: **1 g** Total carbohydrate: **10 g** Dietary fibre: **4 g** Sugars: **0 g** Protein: **5 g**

1 Follow the instructions for Garlicky Hummus (see above), adding the jalapeño pepper with the other spices and briefly pulsing the coriander in at the end. Serve topped with chopped coriander and a sprinkling of crushed chilli flakes, if using.

Yield: 425 g (15 oz)

Ingredients

200 g (7 oz) cooked chickpeas
(1 x 425-g/15-oz tin), rinsed and
drained

1 large garlic clove, minced

2 tablespoons lemon juice

60 g (2½ oz) tahini

2 tablespoons olive oil

1 teaspoon grated lemon zest

1 tablespoon grated fresh turmeric
(or 1 teaspoon ground)

½ teaspoon ground cumin

¼ teaspoon paprika

½ teaspoon sea salt (or to taste)

2–4 tablespoons water (add in to
desired consistency)

chopped fresh flat-leaf parsley,
paprika and a drizzle of olive oil,
to top

Yield: 500 g (1 lb 2 oz)

Ingredients

1 small red pepper

200 g (7 oz) cooked chickpeas
(1 x 425-g/15-oz tin), rinsed
and drained

1 garlic clove, minced

2 tablespoons lemon juice

60 g (2½ oz) tahini

2 tablespoons olive oil, plus extra
to drizzle

½ teaspoon ground cumin

½ teaspoon sea salt (or more)

¼ teaspoon cayenne pepper
(optional)

2 tablespoons fresh flat-leaf parsley,
plus extra to top

sprinkle of paprika, to top

TURMERIC HUMMUS

With cumin, garlic and turmeric all in one place, your
sore muscles will be thanking you for this powerful
anti-inflammatory boost.

Calories: **162** Total fat: **11 g** Saturated fat: **2 g** Total carbohydrate:**10 g**
Dietary fibre: **3 g** Sugars: **0 g** Protein: **5 g**

1   Follow the instructions for Garlicky Hummus (see page 95),
    adding the turmeric with the rest of the spices and seasonings.

ROASTED RED PEPPER HUMMUS

For those times when you need just a light bite to carry you
through, reach for this colourful hummus. The roasted red
pepper adds vitamin C – and parsley is an excellent detoxifier.

Calories: **144** Total fat: **10 g** Saturated fat: **1 g** Total carbohydrate: **10 g**
Dietary fibre: **3 g** Sugars: **1 g** Protein: **5 g**

1   Roast the red pepper by placing it directly on a gas stove or
    grill until the skin is completely blackened. Peel and remove
    seeds from the red pepper under cold water. Roughly chop
    into pieces.

2   Follow the instructions for Garlicky Hummus (see page 95),
    adding the roasted red pepper with the chickpeas and
    pulsing in the parsley at the end. Top with parsley,
    paprika and olive oil.

Opposite, from top: Spiced Roasted Carrot Hummus, page 98;
Roasted Beetroot Dip with Walnuts, Orange and Mint, page 102,
and Classic Guacamole, page 99

Try This

Hummus Jar
Fill the bottom of a mason jar with a serving of any of the
hummus variations, then simply add some sliced veggies for
a healthy pick-me-up snack that is ready to grab and go as
you run out the door.

Yield: 750 g (1¾ lb)

Ingredients

390 g (14 oz) sliced carrots

2 tablespoons olive oil, plus extra
  to serve

½ teaspoon sea salt

¼ teaspoon freshly ground black
  pepper

200 g (7 oz) chickpeas
  (1 x 425-g/15-oz tin), rinsed
  and drained

1 garlic clove, minced

2 tablespoons lemon juice

60 g (2½ oz) tahini

½ teaspoon paprika, plus extra
  to serve

pinch of cayenne pepper

½ teaspoon ground cumin

1 teaspoon grated lemon zest

2–4 tablespoons water, as needed

2 tablespoons fresh coriander, plus
  extra to serve

SPICED ROASTED CARROT HUMMUS

The Moroccan spiced carrots add flavour and beta-carotene to
this bright and beautiful variation. Use your time efficiently by
slicing up your raw veggies while the carrots are roasting.

Calories: **107** Total fat: **7 g** Saturated fat: **1 g** Total carbohydrate: **9 g**
Dietary fibre: **3 g** Sugars: **1 g** Protein: **3 g**

1 Preheat the oven to 200°C (400°F) and line a baking sheet
    with baking paper.

2 Mix the carrots with 1 tablespoon of the olive oil and the
    salt and pepper in a medium bowl. Pour the carrots out
    onto the lined baking sheet and roast in the oven for
    18–20 minutes, until the carrots are golden brown around
    the edges. Stir the carrots once, halfway through roasting.
    Remove from the oven and allow to cool.

3 Follow the instructions for Garlicky Hummus (see page
    95), adding the roasted carrots with the chickpeas, and
    the paprika and cayenne with the rest of the spices and
    seasonings. Pulse in the coriander.

4 Serve with chopped coriander, a sprinkling of paprika and
    a drizzle of olive oil.

 Cook's Note

Hummus Consistency
Homemade hummus will thicken in the fridge. To
reconstitute, add a drop of water or olive oil before serving.

Right: Spiced Roasted Carrot
Hummus

GUACAMOLE

Yield: See each recipe
Serving size: 125 g (4½ oz)
Prep time: 10 minutes
Storage: Best eaten within 24 hours or up to 2 days in the fridge

A true Californian at heart, I've never met an avocado recipe that I didn't like! Avocados are the quintessential example of what is meant by a 'good fat'. With over 25 vital nutrients and minerals, it's no wonder we feel so good from the inside out when we eat avocados!

Yield: 500 g (1 lb 2 oz)

Ingredients

3 avocados, peeled and pitted

2 tablespoons lime juice

½ teaspoon ground cumin

½ teaspoon sea salt (add more to taste)

25 g (1 oz) chopped red onion

½–1 garlic clove, chopped

½ jalapeño pepper, seeds removed and minced (or more to taste)

10 g (½ oz) fresh coriander, finely chopped

CLASSIC GUACAMOLE

Use this simple yet flavourful guacamole to enhance other meals or snacks. Top off the Frittata Cups (see page 80) or put a dollop on some Whole Food Crackers (see page 92). Yum!

Calories: **130** Total fat: **11 g** Saturated fat: **1 g** Total carbohydrate: **9 g** Dietary fibre: **5 g** Sugars: **0 g** Protein: **0 g**

1   Place the scooped-out avocado flesh and lime juice in a large bowl and mash to the desired consistency, leaving some chunks for texture. Season with the cumin and sea salt. Fold in the onion, garlic, jalapeño pepper and coriander and mix. Taste and adjust the seasonings.

2   Serve at room temperature with crisps, or for a healthier option, slice up crunchy vegetables like jicama, carrots and red pepper. Dig in!

Yield: 750 g (1¾ lb)

Ingredients

3 avocados, peeled and pitted

2 tablespoons lime juice

½ teaspoon ground cumin

½ teaspoon sea salt (add more to taste)

25 g (1 oz) chopped red onion

½–1 garlic clove, chopped

½ jalapeño pepper, seeds removed and minced (or more to taste)

10 g (½ oz) fresh coriander, finely chopped

1 medium tomato, finely chopped

SALSA GUACAMOLE

Turn to this salsa guacamole for a refreshing snack on a hot afternoon. Paired with a glass of Spa Water (see page 59), you'll double up on your hydration with the addition of juicy tomato.

Calories: **130** Total fat: **11 g** Saturated fat: **1 g** Total carbohydrate: **9 g** Dietary fibre: **5 g** Sugars: **0 g** Protein: **0 g**

1   Follow the instructions for Classic Guacamole (see above), but gently stir through the chopped tomato at the end. Do not overmix, and make sure to leave chunks of tomato.

 Cook's Note

Storing Guacamole
When storing guacamole in the fridge, place an avocado pit in the container to help prevent the guacamole from browning.

Yield: 750 g (1¾ lb)

Ingredients

drop of olive oil

4 kale leaves, stalks removed

3 avocados, peeled and pitted

2 tablespoons lime juice

½ teaspoon ground cumin

½ teaspoon sea salt (or more to taste)

25 g (1 oz) spring onion, chopped (or red onion)

½–1 garlic clove, chopped (optional)

½ jalapeño pepper, seeds removed and minced (or more depending on desired spiciness)

10 g (½ oz) fresh coriander, finely chopped

Yield: 980 g (2¼ lb)

Ingredients

3 avocados, peeled and pitted

2 tablespoons lime juice

½ teaspoon ground cumin

½ teaspoon sea salt (or more to taste)

25 g (1 oz) red onion, chopped

½–1 garlic clove, chopped

½ jalapeño pepper, seeds removed and minced (or more depending on desired spiciness)

10 g (½ oz) fresh coriander, finely chopped

1 mango, cored and flesh cubed

GREEN ON GREEN GUACAMOLE

The superpowers of kale unite with the beautifying benefits of avocado for an extra-nourishing guac, providing loads of antioxidants to help combat unwanted oxidative stress.

Calories: **136** Total fat: **11 g** Saturated fat: **1 g** Total carbohydrate: **9 g** Dietary fibre: **6 g** Sugars: **1 g** Protein: **1 g**

1 Massage the kale with a drop of olive oil to soften. Slice the leaves into very thin strips, or for less texture, process in a high-speed liquidizer or food processor.

2 Follow the instructions for Classic Guacamole (see page 99), adding the kale at the end.

TROPICAL TREAT GUACAMOLE

If you're someone who needs your sweet and savoury flavours all in one delicious snack, look no further. Mango transports you to the tropics, while giving your body an extra dose of vitamin C.

Calories: **111** Total fat: **9 g** Saturated fat: **1 g** Total carbohydrate: **11 g** Dietary fibre: **4 g** Sugars: **3 g** Protein: **0 g**

1 Follow the instructions for Classic Guacamole (see page 99), adding the cubed mango at the end. Do not overmix, and make sure to leave some chunks of mango.

Right: Green on Green Guacamole

BEETROOT DIPS

Yield: About 500 g (1 lb 2 oz)
Serving size: 60 g (2½ oz)
Prep time: 10 minutes, plus up to 1 hour roasting
Storage: 3 days in an airtight container in the fridge

Beetroot is fantastic for supporting an active lifestyle. From better stamina to improved blood flow and lowered blood pressure, this health-promoting root can't be beat! It's exactly what you need to help you push that extra mile on your run, power up the hill on your bike ride or swim one more lap.

Ingredients

1 medium beetroot
1 tablespoon olive oil, plus extra to drizzle
200 g (7 oz) cooked haricot beans (1 x 425-g/15-oz tin, drained)
3 tablespoons tahini
2 tablespoons lemon juice
1 roasted garlic clove, chopped
1 teaspoon grated lemon zest, plus extra for garnish
½ teaspoon sea salt
1–2 tablespoons water
freshly ground black pepper and sea salt, to taste

ROASTED BEETROOT AND HARICOT BEAN DIP

Creamy and protein-packed thanks to the haricot beans, this dip can be spread on a cracker (see page 92) or served with sliced veggies.

Calories: **124** Total fat: **6 g** Saturated fat: **1 g** Total carbohydrate: **12 g** Dietary fibre: **3 g** Sugars: **1 g** Protein: **6 g**

1 Preheat the oven to 200°C (400°F).

2 Cut off the top and bottom of the beetroot and scrub the root clean. Place the beetroot on a baking sheet and drizzle with a touch of olive oil. Bake for about 35–40 minutes, until tender and easily pierced with a knife or fork; the time can vary, but start checking after 30 minutes. Once the beetroot has cooled to room temperature, peel off the skin and coarsely chop.

3 Place the beetroot in a food processor and process until mostly smooth. Add the haricot beans and process until the mixture becomes creamy. Add the remaining ingredients, except the olive oil and water, and mix until smooth.

4 Slowly drizzle in the olive oil and pulse. If the mixture is too thick, add 1–2 tablespoons water to achieve desired consistency. Adjust seasonings and garnish with lemon zest before serving.

Ingredients

3 medium beetroot, roasted
2 tablespoons tahini
2 tablespoons pine nuts
2 tablespoons lemon juice
1 garlic clove (or more to taste)
1 teaspoon ground cumin
½ teaspoon sea salt
10 g (½ oz) fresh parsley
1–2 tablespoons water, as needed
sea salt and freshly ground black pepper, to taste

ROASTED BEETROOT DIP WITH PINE NUTS AND PARSLEY

When you need a savoury bite to gear up for an afternoon filled with errands or to take you through to the next stage of your workout, reach for this dip.

Calories: **81** Total fat: **5 g** Saturated fat: **1 g** Total carbohydrate: **6 g** Dietary fibre: **2 g** Sugars: **3 g** Protein: **3 g**

1 Follow the instructions for the Roasted Beetroot and Haricot Bean Dip (see above), but reserve the parsley until the end – after the mixture is smooth and creamy, add the parsley and pulse to incorporate, leaving some texture.

Ingredients

3 medium beetroot, roasted

50 g (2 oz) walnuts

2 tablespoons orange juice

½ teaspoon sea salt

2 tablespoons fresh mint, coarsely chopped

1 teaspoon grated orange zest

1 tablespoon olive oil

1–2 tablespoons water if needed

freshly ground black pepper, to taste

ROASTED BEETROOT DIP WITH WALNUTS, ORANGE AND MINT

I came up with this recipe after falling in love with a salad that had all of these ingredients. The walnuts create a creamy texture, while the orange and mint blend with the beetroot for a delicious combination full of heart-healthy goodness.

Calories: **104** Total fat: **9 g** Saturated fat: **1 g** Total carbohydrate: **6 g** Dietary fibre: **2 g** Sugars: **3 g** Protein: **2 g**

1 Roast the beetroot as instructed on page 101.

2 While the beetroot are cooling, place the walnuts in a food processor and process to a smooth texture.

3 Continue adding the ingredients and blending as instructed in the Roasted Beetroot and Haricot Bean Dip on page 101, but reserve the mint and orange zest until the end. When the mixture is smooth and creamy, add the mint and orange zest. Pulse to incorporate, while leaving some texture.

Yield: About 225 g (8 oz)

Serving size: 2 tablespoons

Prep time: 10 minutes

Storage: Best eaten within 4 days, store in an airtight container in the fridge

CASHEW CREAM CHEESE

Cream cheese without dairy? It's possible! The secret super ingredient in this recipe is nutritional yeast, which is an excellent source of vitamin B12. Since it can be tricky to obtain sufficient B12 from plant sources, this is a great option for vegans and people who follow a mostly plant-based diet.

Ingredients

175 g (6 oz) cashews, soaked for 2–4 hours, drained, then rinsed (see Cook's Note opposite)

55 ml (2 fl oz) water

2 tablespoons nutritional yeast

½ teaspoon sea salt

1 tablespoon lemon juice

1 small garlic clove (optional)

SIMPLE CASHEW CREAM CHEESE

Simple, but spreadable and tasty, this dairy-free alternative to cream cheese is a fantastic staple to have on hand.

Calories: **123** Total fat: **10 g** Saturated fat: **2 g** Total carbohydrate: **7 g** Dietary fibre: **1 g** Sugars: **1 g** Protein: **4 g**

1 Place all the ingredients in a food processor and process until creamy.

 Cook's Note

Adjust Consistency
Add a drop of water the next day if the cream cheese thickens overnight.

Ingredients

175 g (6 oz) cashews, soaked for 2–4 hours, drained, then rinsed

60 ml (2 fl oz) water

2 tablespoons nutritional yeast

½ teaspoon sea salt

1 tablespoon lemon juice

1 small garlic clove (optional)

2 tablespoons shallots, roughly chopped (green parts only)

SHALLOT CASHEW CREAM CHEESE

Delicate shallots and lemon juice create a fresh, tangy version of this classic flavour.

Calories: **125** Total fat: **10 g** Saturated fat: **2 g** Total carbohydrate: **7 g**
Dietary fibre: **1 g** Sugars: **1 g** Protein: **4 g**

1   Follow the instructions for Simple Cashew Cream Cheese (see opposite), but reserve the shallots until the end. Scrape down the sides, then add the shallots and pulse until thoroughly incorporated.

Ingredients

175 g (6 oz) cashews, soaked for 2–4 hours, drained, then rinsed

55 ml (2 fl oz) water

2 tablespoons nutritional yeast

½ teaspoon sea salt

1 tablespoon lemon juice

1 small garlic clove (optional)

2 tablespoons sun-dried tomatoes

2 tablespoons fresh basil, roughly chopped

TOMATO BASIL CASHEW CREAM CHEESE

When you want a taste of sunshine, this is the spread for you. Sun-dried tomatoes are packed full of antioxidants and actually contain more vitamin C than raw tomatoes.

Calories: **126** Total fat: **10 g** Saturated fat: **2 g** Total carbohydrate: **7 g**
Dietary fibre: **1 g** Sugars: **1 g** Protein: **4 g**

1   Follow the instructions for Simple Cashew Cream Cheese (see opposite), adding the sun-dried tomatoes with the other ingredients but reserving the basil until the end. Scrape down the sides, then add the basil and pulse until thoroughly incorporated.

Ingredients

175 g (6 oz) cashews, soaked for 2–4 hours, drained, then rinsed

55 ml (2 fl oz) water

2 tablespoons nutritional yeast

½ teaspoon sea salt

1 tablespoon lime juice

1 small garlic clove (optional)

½ teaspoon paprika

½ teaspoon ground cumin

½ jalapeño, seeds removed

10 g (½ oz) fresh coriander

MEXICAN CASHEW CREAM CHEESE

Spice it up with fiesta flavours in this variation – zesty lime, smoky paprika and hot jalapeño.

Calories: **122** Total fat: **9 g** Saturated fat: **2 g** Total carbohydrate: **7 g**
Dietary fibre: **1 g** Sugars: **1 g** Protein: **4 g**

1   Follow the instructions for Simple Cashew Cream Cheese (see opposite), adding the jalapeño with the other ingredients but reserving the coriander until the end. Scrape down the sides, then add the coriander and pulse until thoroughly incorporated.

 Cook's Note

Soak Your Cashews
To make the cream cheese, you will need to soak the cashews in filtered water for 2–4 hours. Once soaked, drain and rinse thoroughly before using.

STUFFED DATES

Yield: 1 date

Serving size: 1 date

Prep time: Under 5 minutes

Storage: Best eaten immediately or stored in an airtight container in the fridge for up to 3 days

If you have only one minute to put together an energizing and satisfying snack, then stuffed dates are your answer. Simply slice open a fresh date, remove the pit and fill the cavity with nut butter. Then, sprinkle with raw cacao nibs, shredded coconut or cinnamon, or enjoy au naturel.

Ingredients

1 pitted Medjool date

1 teaspoon nut butter (see pages 160–162)

¼ teaspoon topping – choose from raw cacao nibs, shredded coconut, ground cinnamon or ground flax seeds (optional)

BASIC STUFFED DATE

Stuffed dates are the perfect grab-and-go snack. With natural sugar (plus fibre and nutrients), it's no wonder that people refer to this fruit as Mother Nature's sweet.

Calories: **98** Total fat: **3 g** Saturated fat: **0 g** Total carbohydrate: **19 g**
Dietary fibre: **2 g** Sugars: **16 g** Protein: **2 g**

1 Slice the date lengthwise, fill with the nut butter and sprinkle on a topping of choice, if desired. Eat immediately or store in the fridge, as the nut butter will soften at room temperature.

Opposite: Stuffed Dates with almond butter

 Try This

Whole Nut Stuffed Date
Instead of nut butter, place a whole nut inside the date – pecans and almonds are great options.

BERRY-LICIOUS CHIA JAM

Yield: About 150 g (5 oz)
Serving size: 1 tablespoon
Prep time: 10–15 minutes, plus
1 hour chilling (or more)
Storage: Up to 1 week in an airtight
container in the fridge

Layered in parfaits, served with warm muffins, mixed into banana ice cream or stirred into overnight oats, chia seed jam is both delicious and easy to prepare. Super-powered chia seeds thicken the jam and add a nutritional punch with protein, fibre and omega-3s.

Ingredients

215 g (7½ oz) blueberries (fresh or thawed frozen)

1 tablespoon lemon juice

60 ml (2 fl oz) water (only if using fresh berries)

2 tablespoons maple syrup (or honey)

1 teaspoon lemon zest

2 tablespoons chia seeds

LEMONY BLUEBERRY CHIA JAM

Supercharge your jam with blueberries, which are rich in vitamins K and C, fibre and manganese – all great for heart and brain health.

Calories: **30** Total fat: **1 g** Saturated fat: **0 g** Total carbohydrate: **5 g**
Dietary fibre: **1 g** Sugars: **3 g** Protein: **1 g**

1   Mash the thawed frozen or fresh berries in a medium bowl with a fork, and add the lemon juice. Add water if using fresh berries.

2   Place the mashed berries and maple syrup in a small saucepan. Bring to a boil over high heat, then reduce to a simmer. Cook for 4–5 minutes, stirring frequently. Remove the saucepan from the heat, add the lemon zest and mix well. Add the chia seeds, stir and leave to cool.

3   Once cooled, place the thickened jam in a mason jar or airtight container and chill for 1 hour before serving.

Ingredients

185 g (6½ oz) raspberries (fresh or thawed frozen)

55 ml (2 fl oz) water (only if using fresh berries)

2 tablespoons maple syrup (honey works well too)

2 tablespoons chia seeds

RASPBERRY CHIA JAM

This naturally sweet jam pairs beautifully with any of the DIY nut butters (see pages 160–162) for a whole food version of peanut butter and jelly.

Calories: **28** Total fat: **1 g** Saturated fat: **0 g** Total carbohydrate: **4 g**
Dietary fibre: **2 g** Sugars: **2 g** Protein: **1 g**

1   Follow the instructions for the Lemony Blueberry Chia Jam (see above).

Ingredients

215 g (7½ oz) blackberries (fresh or thawed frozen)

55 ml (2 fl oz) water (only if using fresh berries)

2 tablespoons maple syrup

½ teaspoon pure vanilla extract

2 tablespoons chia seeds

BLACKBERRY VANILLA CHIA JAM

Stir in vanilla as the jam cools for an extra hit of flavour in this sweet and antioxidant-rich blackberry spread.

Calories: **28** Total fat: **1 g** Saturated fat: **0 g** Total carbohydrate: **4 g**
Dietary fibre: **2 g** Sugars: **2 g** Protein: **1 g**

1   Follow the instructions for the Lemony Blueberry Chia Jam (see above), but reserve the vanilla extract until after the jam is cooling and add prior to mixing in the chia seeds.

> 🥄 **Try This**
>
> **Added Citrus Zest**
> Try adding a citrus note to the Raspberry Chia Jam with the zest and juice of an orange or lemon.

Opposite: Raspberry Chia Jam

ROASTED CHICKPEAS

Yield: 200 g (7 oz)
Serving size: 75 g (3 oz)
Prep time: 10 minutes, plus 35–40 minutes baking and 10 minutes cooling
Storage: Best eaten on the first day but can be stored at room temperature for up to 3 days

Also known as garbanzo beans, chickpeas are an excellent source of fibre and plant-based protein, with the added health benefit of keeping cholesterol levels in check. If purchasing tinned chickpeas, always choose organic brands. Or, ideally, avoid tins altogether by soaking and cooking your own chickpeas. It's easier than you think!

Ingredients

200 g (7 oz) chickpeas (1 x 425-g/15-oz tin), rinsed and drained
1 teaspoon paprika
1 teaspoon ground cumin
1 teaspoon ground cinnamon
½ teaspoon sea salt
1 tablespoon olive oil

SEA SALT, PAPRIKA, CUMIN AND CINNAMON CHICKPEAS

This simple mix creates an incredibly satisfying whole food snack that can be eaten by the handful or tossed into trail mixes, salads or soups.

Calories: **163** Total fat: **7 g** Saturated fat: **1 g** Total carbohydrate: **20 g**
Dietary fibre: **7 g** Sugars: **0 g** Protein: **6 g**

1 Preheat the oven to 190°C (375°F) and line a large rimmed baking sheet with baking paper.

2 Pat the chickpeas dry, and make sure they are completely dry before roasting. Place them in a medium-sized bowl. Mix the dry spices together in a separate small bowl until well combined.

3 Pour the olive oil over the chickpeas and stir. Add the spice mix and roll the chickpeas around in the bowl to make sure they are evenly coated.

4 Spread the chickpeas out on the lined baking sheet in a single layer and roast for 20 minutes. Stir the chickpeas and cook for an additional 15–20 minutes, until the chickpeas are golden brown. Allow to cool on the baking sheet for 10 minutes to allow the chickpeas to crisp up before serving.

Ingredients

200 g (7 oz) chickpeas (1 x 425-g/15-oz tin)
2 teaspoons curry powder
1 teaspoon turmeric
½ teaspoon sea salt
1 tablespoon coconut oil
10 g (½ oz) chopped fresh coriander

COCONUT CURRY CHICKPEAS

The perfect answer to a mid-afternoon slump, these crunchy and crispy chickpeas are big on flavour and nutrition.

Calories: **164** Total fat: **7 g** Saturated fat: **4 g** Total carbohydrate: **20 g**
Dietary fibre: **6 g** Sugars: **0 g** Protein: **6 g**

1 Follow the instructions for the Sea Salt, Paprika, Cumin and Cinnamon Chickpeas (see above), but stir through the coriander to lightly coat the chickpeas once they are out of the oven and cooling.

Ingredients

200 g (7 oz) chickpeas
(1 x 425-g/15-oz tin)
1 tablespoon olive oil
1 tablespoon lime juice
1 teaspoon chilli powder
½ teaspoon sea salt
1–2 teaspoons grated lime zest

CHILLI LIME CHICKPEAS

I love the combination of zesty lime and the gentle heat of chilli powder in this recipe. Perfect for an afternoon protein boost.

Calories: **151** Total fat: **7 g** Saturated fat: **1 g** Total carbohydrate: **19 g**
Dietary fibre: **6 g** Sugars: **0 g** Protein: **6 g**

1   Follow the instructions for the Sea Salt, Paprika, Cumin and Cinnamon Chickpeas (see opposite), but add the lime zest to lightly coat the chickpeas once they are out of the oven and cooling.

Ingredients

200 g (7 oz) chickpeas
(1 x 425-g/15-oz tin)
1 tablespoon olive oil
3 tablespoons nutritional yeast
1 tablespoon lemon juice
½ teaspoon sea salt
1 teaspoon minced garlic
⅛ teaspoon freshly ground black pepper
1 teaspoon grated lemon zest

PEPPER AND GARLIC CHICKPEAS

Skip the croutons and toss these onto the Moroccan Spiced Tomato Soup for a hearty addition to this light meal (see page 48).

Calories: **180** Total fat: **7 g** Saturated fat: **1 g** Total carbohydrate: **22 g**
Dietary fibre: **7 g** Sugars: **0 g** Protein: **9 g**

1   Follow the instructions for the Sea Salt, Paprika, Cumin and Cinnamon Chickpeas (see opposite), but add the lemon zest to lightly coat the chickpeas once they are out of the oven and cooling.

Below: Sea Salt, Paprika, Cumin and Cinnamon Chickpeas

SPICED NUTS

Yield: About 275 g (10 oz)

Serving size: 60 g (2½ oz)

Prep time: For almonds, 5 minutes, plus 20 minutes baking; for cashews, 5 minutes, plus 10–12 minutes baking

Storage: Up to 7 days at room temperature in an airtight container

Bored with handfuls of raw almonds or cashews? I've got you covered. The healing spices in these simple roasted recipes take protein-packed nuts to the next level. Add these to soups, salads, trail mixes or light meals and snacks for a boost of protein and healthy fat. Or grab a handful with a piece of fruit to tide you over until your next meal.

Ingredients

350 g (12 oz) cashews

1 tablespoon coconut oil, melted

1 tablespoon maple syrup (may use more depending on desired level of sweetness)

½ teaspoon cayenne pepper

1 teaspoon sweet curry powder

½ teaspoon sea salt

25 g (1 oz) dried shredded coconut

SPICY COCONUT CURRY CASHEWS

Bursting with both sweet and savoury flavours, this variation is my personal favourite. Containing turmeric, curry powder is another natural way to add the anti-inflammatory benefits of curcumin to your diet.

Calories: **170** Total fat: **13 g** Saturated fat: **4 g** Total carbohydrate: **6 g** Dietary fibre: **1 g** Sugars: **3 g** Protein: **5 g**

1 Preheat the oven to 170°C (325°F) and line a large rimmed baking sheet with baking paper.

2 Place the cashews in a medium-sized bowl. Mix the coconut oil and maple syrup in a small bowl and pour it over the cashews. Toss to evenly coat the nuts.

3 Mix the cayenne pepper, curry powder and sea salt together in a small bowl, then add to the nut mixture and toss to coat. Add the shredded coconut and mix.

4 Spread the nuts out on the baking sheet in an even layer and bake for 10–12 minutes, stirring and checking to make sure the nuts don't burn after 8 minutes. Remove from the oven once golden brown. Allow to cool and crisp up before serving.

Right: Spicy Coconut Curry Cashews

VANILLA ORANGE CASHEWS

Ingredients

350 g (12 oz) cashews

1 tablespoon coconut oil

1 teaspoon pure vanilla extract (or vanilla seeds from a bean)

1 tablespoon freshly squeezed orange juice

1 tablespoon honey

1 tablespoon grated orange zest

¼ teaspoon sea salt

For a sweet option, this combination of citrus-fresh orange and fragrant vanilla works beautifully with the cashews.

Calories: **186** Total fat: **14 g** Saturated fat: **4 g** Total carbohydrate: **11 g**
Dietary fibre: **1 g** Sugars: **4 g** Protein: **5 g**

1 Follow the instructions for Spicy Coconut Curry Cashews (see opposite), covering the cashews with the oil mixture first. In a separate bowl, mix the orange juice and honey together, then toss the cashews in the mixture, before finally adding the zest and salt. Adjust seasoning according to taste. Bake, then cool before serving.

'CHEESY' CASHEWS

Ingredients

350 g (12 oz) cashews

1 tablespoon olive oil

2 tablespoons nutritional yeast

1 teaspoon paprika

1 teaspoon sea salt

The nutritional yeast in this recipe gives the cashews a delightful cheesy flavour, but without any cheese.

Calories: **161** Total fat: **12 g** Saturated fat: **2 g** Total carbohydrate: **8 g**
Dietary fibre: **1 g** Sugars: **2 g** Protein: **5 g**

1 Follow the instructions for Spicy Coconut Curry Cashews (see opposite), covering the cashews with the olive oil first. In a separate bowl, mix the dry ingredients together, then toss the dried seasonings over the cashews and adjust seasoning according to taste. Bake, then cool before serving.

SPICY MIXED NUTS

Ingredients

175 g (6 oz) almonds

50 g (2 oz) pecans

50 g (2 oz) walnuts

1 tablespoon olive oil

¼–½ teaspoon cayenne pepper (depending on desired spiciness)

½ teaspoon ground cumin

1 teaspoon chilli powder

½ teaspoon sea salt

You can't go wrong with a powerful combination of calcium-rich almonds, heart-healthy pecans and antioxidant-packed walnuts.

Calories: **199** Total fat: **19 g** Saturated fat: **5 g** Total carbohydrate: **5 g**
Dietary fibre: **3 g** Sugars: **1 g** Protein: **5 g**

1 Preheat the oven to 325°F (170°C) and line a large rimmed baking sheet with baking paper.

2 Place the nuts in a medium-sized bowl, pour in the oil and toss to coat.

3 Mix all the dry seasonings together in a small bowl. Add to the nut mixture and stir to coat evenly.

4 Spread the nuts out on the baking sheet in a single layer and bake for 18–20 minutes, stirring about halfway through and making sure the nuts don't burn. Remove from the oven, once slightly brown. Allow to cool to crisp up before serving.

Ingredients

350 g (12 oz) almonds

1 tablespoon tamari (gluten-free soy sauce)

2 teaspoons honey

2 teaspoons toasted sesame oil

½ teaspoon wasabi powder

½ teaspoon ground ginger

½–1 teaspoon chilli pepper flakes

½ teaspoon sea salt

SWEET AND SPICY ASIAN-INSPIRED ALMONDS

Eating whole roasted almonds is a good way to get all the delicious goodness from the almond skin, which contains heart-healthy flavonoids.

Calories: **200** Total fat: **16 g** Saturated fat: **1 g** Total carbohydrate: **8 g**
Dietary fibre: **4 g** Sugars: **3 g** Protein: **6 g**

1   Follow the instructions for Spicy Mixed Nuts (see page 111), mixing the tamari and honey before adding to coat the almonds at step 2. Adjust seasoning according to taste.

Ingredients

350 g (12 oz) almonds

1 tablespoon tomato paste

1 tablespoon olive oil

1½ teaspoons dried basil

1½ teaspoons dried oregano

½ teaspoon granulated garlic powder

½ teaspoon granulated onion powder

1 teaspoon sea salt

PIZZA ON THE RUN

Transport yourself to Rome with the flavours of tomato, basil and oregano.

Calories: **225** Total fat: **20 g** Saturated fat: **2 g** Total carbohydrate: **8 g**
Dietary fibre: **4 g** Sugars: **2 g** Protein: **8 g**

1   Follow the instructions for Spicy Mixed Nuts (see page 111), mixing the tomato paste and olive oil before adding to coat the almonds at step 2. Adjust seasoning according to taste.

Ingredients

350 g (12 oz) almonds

1 tablespoon melted coconut oil

1½ tablespoons maple syrup

½ teaspoon pure vanilla extract

½ teaspoon sea salt

1 tablespoon raw cacao or cocoa powder

CACAO-DUSTED ALMONDS

An excellent blood sugar stabilizing choice to satisfy a mid-afternoon chocolate craving.

Calories: **208** Total fat: **17 g** Saturated fat: **3 g** Total carbohydrate: **9 g**
Dietary fibre: **4 g** Sugars: **2 g** Protein: **6 g**

1   Follow the instructions for Spicy Mixed Nuts (see page 111), mixing the melted coconut oil and maple syrup before adding to coat the almonds at step 2. Reserve the cacao powder until after baking, and dust the nuts to coat evenly.

Try This

Mexican Chocolate
Make a spicy Mexican-inspired version of the Cacao-Dusted Almonds by adding ¼ teaspoon cayenne pepper, ¼ teaspoon ground nutmeg and 1 teaspoon ground cinnamon before putting the almonds in the oven.

ENERGY BARS

A staple in every active person's larder, bars are a quick pick-me-up when you need energy. The problem is that ready-made varieties are often packed with refined sugars, additives and other hidden ingredients. By making your own bars, you'll be certain that you're getting all the right nutrients to support your energy needs while leaving the less-healthy ingredients out. And the best part? They couldn't be easier to make.

Chocolatey Oat and Nut Breakfast Bars, page 116

BREAKFAST BARS

Yield: 12 bars

Serving size: 1 bar

Prep time: 10–15 minutes, plus 25 minutes cooking

Storage: Best kept in an airtight container in the fridge for 4 days, at room temperature for 1 day, or in the freezer for longer storage

Whether you're rushing out the door without time to sit down and eat, or need a portable source of nourishment to munch on after your 6 A.M. workout, the breakfast bar is the perfect staple to keep on hand. These bars are packed with slow-release carbs, healthy fats from creamy nut butter and crunchy nuts, plus a whole lot of flavour. Don't let the name fool you – these breakfast bars can be enjoyed any time of day.

Ingredients

200 g (7 oz) mashed banana
150 g (5 oz) cashew butter
½ teaspoon pure vanilla extract
110 g (4 oz) cashews
40 g (1½ oz) sunflower seeds
½ teaspoon sea salt
100 g (3½ oz) dried blueberries
100 g (3½ oz) rolled oats

BLUEBERRY CASHEW BREAKFAST BARS

Breakfast isn't boring when it involves the winning combination of blueberries and cashews. With a serving of satisfying oats, your morning will be off to a great start.

Calories: **165** Total fat: **9 g** Saturated fat: **2 g** Total carbohydrate: **18 g**
Dietary fibre: **3 g** Sugars: **6 g** Protein: **5 g**

1   Preheat the oven to 180°C (350°F) and line a 20.5 x 20.5-cm (8 x 8-in) baking tin with baking paper.

2   Place the mashed banana and cashew butter in a small saucepan and gently heat. Stir for 2–3 minutes, until well combined. Turn off the heat and set aside. Once cooled slightly, add the vanilla extract and mix.

3   Place the cashews in a food processor and pulse to roughly chop – this can also be done with a sharp knife by hand, if preferred.

4   Transfer the nuts to a bowl and mix in the sunflower seeds, salt, dried blueberries and oats. Add the banana and cashew butter mixture and mix.

5   Press the batter into the prepared pan and use another sheet of baking paper on top to press and flatten evenly. Bake uncovered for 20–25 minutes, until golden brown around the edges. Allow to cool before cutting into bars or squares.

Ingredients

125 g (4½ oz) almond butter
200 g (7 oz) mashed banana
½ teaspoon pure vanilla extract
2 tablespoons orange juice
40 g (1½) almonds
60 g (2½ oz) pecans
60 g (2½ oz) dried cranberries
½ teaspoon ground cinnamon
pinch of ground nutmeg
1 teaspoon grated fresh ginger (or
    ¼ teaspoon ground ginger)
½ teaspoon sea salt
100 g (3½ oz) rolled oats
1 teaspoon grated orange zest

ORANGE CRANBERRY SPICE BREAKFAST BARS

To power through your morning run, this spiced breakfast bar makes for a perfect pre-workout snack.

Calories: **168** Total fat: **12 g** Saturated fat: **1 g** Total carbohydrate: **14 g**
Dietary fibre: **4 g** Sugars: **4 g** Protein: **5 g**

1   Follow the instructions for the Blueberry Cashew Breakfast Bars (see above), adding the orange juice with the vanilla extract. After roughly chopping the almonds and pecans at step 3, add the dried cranberries to the food processor and pulse to roughly chop. Stir the orange zest through the mixture last, just before pressing the batter into the prepared tin.

Opposite: Orange Cranberry Spice Breakfast Bars

Yield: 16 bars
Serving size: 1 bar

Ingredients

25 g (1 oz) shredded unsweetened
   coconut

2 tablespoons hemp seeds

2 tablespoons ground flax seeds

1 tablespoon chia seeds

1 teaspoon ground cinnamon

½ teaspoon sea salt

135 g (4¾ oz) rolled oats

75 g (3 oz) almonds

25 g (1 oz) walnuts

25 g (1 oz) pecans

135 g (4¾ oz) pitted Medjool dates

2 tablespoons almond butter

2 tablespoons coconut oil, softened

1 teaspoon pure vanilla extract

½ teaspoon almond extract
   (optional)

40 g (1½ oz) mini chocolate chips

CHOCOLATEY OAT AND NUT BREAKFAST BARS

Chocolate for breakfast? Why not! The almonds boast a hefty dose of healthy fats and vitamin E, while the oats give you a good serving of fibre to help keep your blood sugar in check.

Calories: **166** Total fat: **9 g** Saturated fat: **4 g** Total carbohydrate: **20 g**
Dietary fibre: **3 g** Sugars: **10 g** Protein: **4 g**

1   Preheat the oven to 170°C (325°F) and line a 23 x 12.5-cm (9 x 5-in) baking tin with baking paper.

2   Mix together the shredded coconut, hemp seeds, ground flax seeds, chia seeds, cinnamon and sea salt in a large bowl. Place the oats in a food processor and process until coarse but not smooth. Add to the seed mixture.

3   Add the nuts to the food processor and process until the nuts are in small pieces but not a flour. Add the nuts to the bowl with the oat and seed mixture.

4   Add the dates, almond butter and coconut oil to the food processor and process until smooth. Add the vanilla extract and almond extract, if using, and pulse together.

5   Fold the date mixture into the bowl with the nuts and oats and mix well – you can use your hands to incorporate all the ingredients. Add the chocolate chips and mix through.

6   Place the mixture into the prepared baking tin and use another sheet of baking paper to press and flatten evenly. Bake for 18–20 minutes, until the tops are golden brown.

7   Remove from the oven and allow to cool. Place in the fridge to set for at least 1 hour before slicing into 16 bars and serving.

 Cook's Note

Chopping Nuts and Seeds
Roughly chop nuts or seeds by placing them in a food processor and pulsing just a few times, or chop by hand on a cutting board with a sharp knife.

CHEWY POWER BARS

Yield: 12 bars

Serving size: 1 bar

Prep time: 10 minutes, plus 1 hour to set

Storage: Up to 5 days in an airtight container in the fridge, or freeze for up to 1 month

These bars have it all – delicious flavours, a combination of satisfying textures (chewy and crunchy in one bar) and enough staying power to fuel an active lifestyle. An all-natural source of portable energy using raw ingredients, these chewy power bars couldn't be easier to make … or eat!

Ingredients

50 g (2 oz) rolled oats

200 g (7 oz) pitted Medjool dates

60 g (2½ oz) unsweetened natural peanut butter

1 teaspoon pure vanilla extract

½ teaspoon sea salt

110 g (4 oz) dried cherries

75 g (3 oz) almonds, roughly chopped

PB AND J POWER BARS

My sons ask for these peanut butter and jelly bars on repeat. The oats, dried fruit and nuts provide a great balance of macronutrients.

Calories: **166** Total fat: **6 g** Saturated fat: **1 g** Total carbohydrate: **26 g** Dietary fibre: **3 g** Sugars: **17 g** Protein: **3 g**

1 Line a 23 x 13-cm (9 x 5-in) loaf pan with baking paper.

2 Place the oats in a food processor and pulse until they are coarsely chopped but still have some texture – do not overprocess or create a powder.

3 Add the other ingredients, except for the dried cherries and almonds. Process until the mixture starts to stick together and clump on the sides of the bowl. Add the dried cherries and pulse a few times.

4 Transfer the mixture to a medium-sized bowl and add the roughly chopped almonds. Place a piece of baking paper on top of the mixture and use your hands to incorporate the nuts and dried fruit with the other ingredients.

5 Transfer the mixture to the prepared loaf pan and use another sheet of baking paper on top to press and flatten evenly into the pan. Refrigerate for 1 hour before cutting into 12 equal-sized bars.

 Cook's Note

Buying Dried Fruits
When buying dried fruits, try to select varieties labelled as 'unsulphured'.

🧑‍🍳 **Cook's Note**

Soak Your Fruit
If your dried fruit is particularly hard, simply soak it before using. Place the dried fruit in a bowl of warm water and leave to soak for 5–10 minutes, then drain and let it dry completely before using it in the recipe.

Ingredients

50 g (2 oz) rolled oats

200 g (7 oz) pitted Medjool dates

60 g (2½ oz) almond butter

25 g (1 oz) shredded coconut

40 g (1½ oz) cacao powder or unsweetened cocoa powder

1 teaspoon pure vanilla extract

½ teaspoon sea salt

75 g (3 oz) almonds, roughly chopped

Ingredients

50 g (2 oz) rolled oats

200 g (7 oz) pitted Medjool dates

60 g (2½ oz) sunflower seed butter

1 teaspoon pure vanilla extract

½ teaspoon sea salt

75 g (3 oz) cashews, roughly chopped

75 g (3 oz) dried apricots, roughly chopped

Ingredients

50 g (2 oz) rolled oats

200 g (7 oz) pitted Medjool dates

60 g (2½ oz) cashew butter

75 g (3 oz) pumpkin seeds, roughly chopped

1 teaspoon ground cinnamon

½ teaspoon sea salt

1 teaspoon grated orange zest

60 g (2½ oz) dried cranberries

COCONUT, ALMOND AND CHOCOLATE POWER BARS

Reminiscent of a favourite chocolate bar, the coconut, chocolate and almond threesome will win you over in taste and nutrition.

Calories: **161** Total fat: **9 g** Saturated fat: **1 g** Total carbohydrate: **23 g** Dietary fibre: **4 g** Sugars: **15 g** Protein: **4 g**

1   Follow the instructions for the PB and J Power Bars (see page 117), reserving just the almonds at step 3.

APRICOT AND SUNFLOWER POWER BARS

I've got a secret stash of these in my freezer to enjoy before I go for a run. I'm always trying to find ways to pump up my iron stores, and dried apricots are a rich source of this mineral.

Calories: **152** Total fat: **5 g** Saturated fat: **1 g** Total carbohydrate: **25 g** Dietary fibre: **3 g** Sugars: **6 g** Protein: **3 g**

1   Follow the instructions for the PB and J Power Bars (see page 117). Chop the apricots by hand before mixing into the combined ingredients.

CRANBERRY PUMPKIN POWER BARS

With flavours reminding you of spiced pumpkin pie and tangy cranberry sauce, you might forget that these bars are healthy!

Calories: **139** Total fat: **5 g** Saturated fat: **1 g** Total carbohydrate: **22 g** Dietary fibre: **3 g** Sugars: **15 g** Protein: **3 g**

1   Follow the instructions for the PB and J Power Bars (see page 117), but pulse in the orange zest at the end with the dried cranberries. There are no chopped nuts to add at step 4 for this variation.

Opposite: PB and J Power Bars, page 117

RAW FRUIT AND NUT BARS

Need something to carry you from the office to your evening workout and the meetings in-between? Try these grain-free bars for sustaining, slow-release energy. A mixture of sweet dates, crunchy nuts and smooth nut butter makes the perfect whole food base with added nutrients – and flavour – from spices and dried fruits.

Yield: 8 bars

Serving size: 1 bar

Prep time: 10 minutes, plus 1 hour chilling

Storage: Up to 5 days in an airtight container in the fridge or 1 month in the freezer

FUDGY BROWNIE BARS

Chocolate lovers rejoice. If you crave something decadent that will keep your energy levels balanced, these fudgy brownie bars are the real deal.

Calories: **188** Total fat: **12 g** Saturated fat: **1 g** Total carbohydrate: **22 g**
Dietary fibre: **5 g** Sugars: **15 g** Protein: **5 g**

Ingredients

75 g (3 oz) almonds

50 g (2 oz) walnuts

60 g (2½ oz) pitted Medjool dates (soaked if necessary, see Cook's Note, page 118)

1 tablespoon almond butter

25 g (1 oz) raw cacao powder or unsweetened cocoa powder

2 tablespoons cacao nibs

½ teaspoon pure vanilla extract

pinch of sea salt

1 tablespoon crushed nuts, to top

1 Line a 23 x 12.5-cm (9 x 5-in) loaf tin with baking paper.

2 Place the nuts in a food processor and pulse until finely chopped, with some small chunks remaining. Add the rest of the ingredients, except the nuts for topping, and pulse until the ingredients start to stick together. Do not process until smooth, as the texture helps the bars hold together.

3 Transfer the mixture to the prepared loaf tin and use a sheet of baking paper on top to press and flatten evenly using the palm of your hand. Sprinkle the crushed nuts on top, then cover the pan with baking paper or cling film. Place the covered bars in the fridge for 1 hour before slicing into 8 individual bars.

APRICOT VANILLA CASHEW BARS

Reach for one of these bars when you get to the top of the mountain on your hike. The apricots provide a great source of dietary fibre and iron, while the creamy cashews are sure to keep you satisfied until you hit the bottom.

Calories: **146** Total fat: **7 g** Saturated fat: **1 g** Total carbohydrate: **19 g**
Dietary fibre: **2 g** Sugars: **13 g** Protein: **3 g**

Ingredients

175 g (6 oz) cashews

150 g (5 oz) dried apricots

25 g (1 oz) pitted Medjool dates

1 tablespoon cashew butter

1 teaspoon pure vanilla extract

pinch of sea salt

shredded coconut to top (optional)

1 Follow the instructions for the Fudgy Brownie Bars (see above), topping the bars with shredded coconut if desired.

Opposite: Apricot Vanilla Cashew Bars

Ingredients

175 g (6 oz) almonds
125 g (4½ oz) dried cherries
40 g (1½ oz) pitted Medjool dates
1 tablespoon almond butter
½ teaspoon pure vanilla extract
pinch of sea salt

SPICED CHERRY PIE BARS

Dried cherries are not only rich in antioxidants, but they also support vision and are good for your skin. The almonds and almond butter will help keep you full during a busy day.

Calories: **178** Total fat: **9 g** Saturated fat: **1 g** Total carbohydrate: **21 g**
Dietary fibre: **4 g** Sugars: **12 g** Protein: **4 g**

1   Follow the instructions for the Fudgy Brownie Bars (see page 120).

Ingredients

175 g (6 oz) cashews
135 g (4¾ oz) pitted Medjool dates
2 tablespoons lemon juice
1 tablespoon coconut butter (cashew butter also works)
1 teaspoon grated lemon zest
40 g (1½ oz) shredded coconut, plus 1 tablespoon to top
½ teaspoon pure vanilla extract
pinch of sea salt

LUSCIOUS LEMON BARS

Mixing in lemon gives you a sweet and zesty pick-me-up and provides a hefty dose of vitamin C.

Calories: **176** Total fat: **9 g** Saturated fat: **4 g** Total carbohydrate: **22 g**
Dietary fibre: **3 g** Sugars: **16 g** Protein: **3 g**

1   Follow the instructions for the Fudgy Brownie Bars (see page 120), but save the tablespoon of shredded coconut to top the bars before chilling.

Ingredients

75 g (3 oz) cashews
40 g (1½ oz) pecans
40 g (1½ oz) macadamia nuts
60 g (2½ oz) dried strawberries
60 g (2½ oz) dried cranberries
40 g (1½ oz) pitted Medjool dates
1 tablespoon cashew butter
½ teaspoon pure vanilla extract
1 teaspoon grated lemon zest

STRAWBERRY SHORTCAKE BARS

The name alone says it all! Sweet strawberries and tangy cranberries unite with the wholesome goodness of macadamia nuts, which add heart-healthy monounsaturated fatty acids.

Calories: **133** Total fat: **9 g** Saturated fat: **1 g** Total carbohydrate: **13 g**
Dietary fibre: **3 g** Sugars: **7 g** Protein: **3 g**

1   Follow the instructions for the Fudgy Brownie Bars (see page 120), adding the lemon zest to the food processor at the end.

 Try This

Extra Strawberry
For intense strawberry flavour in the Strawberry Shortcake Bars, use fewer dried cranberries and more dried strawberries.

ENERGY BALLS

An easy, portable option, energy balls are packed full of whole food goodness. Naturally sweet dates contain essential nutrients, vitamins and minerals to help keep you healthy and active. Add in protein-rich nuts and seeds with a dash of healing spices, and you have everything you need to fuel your body while still feeling satisfied.

Zesty Orange Chocolate Energy Balls, page 125

CHOCOLATE ENERGY BALLS

A base of dates, cacao powder and nuts make these bite-sized balls the perfect snack to grab before a workout or enjoy as a dessert. While the combination of raw cacao and dates provides lots of energizing nutrients, these tasty energy balls are equally satisfying when you just need a little something to lift you up.

Yield: 20 2.5-cm (1-in) balls

Serving size: 1 energy ball

Prep time: 10–15 minutes, plus 1 hour chilling

Storage: Up to 3 days in an airtight container in the fridge or 1 month in the freezer

Ingredients

100 g (3½ oz) walnuts (can use almonds, cashews, or pecans)

100 g (3½ oz) pitted Medjool dates

25 g (1½ oz) unsweetened cocoa powder or raw cacao powder

pinch of sea salt

1 teaspoon pure vanilla extract

cocoa powder, raw cacao powder and/or shredded coconut, for dusting

DECADENT CHOCOLATE BROWNIE ENERGY BALLS

Craving a gooey brownie? Try sinking your teeth into one of these ultra-chocolatey energy balls. These bites will keep your blood sugar in check and your body happy in-between meals.

Calories: **69** Total fat: **5 g** Saturated fat: **0 g** Total carbohydrate: **8 g** Dietary fibre: **1 g** Sugars: **6 g** Protein: **1 g**

1 Place the nuts in a food processor and process until crumbly but still with a bit of texture. Add the dates, cocoa or cacao powder, sea salt and vanilla extract, and blend again.

2 With slightly wet hands, roll the mixture into 2.5-cm (1-in) balls. If the mixture is too sticky to handle, place in the freezer for about 15–20 minutes until firm enough to roll.

3 Lightly cover each truffle with your choice of dusting ingredient and place them on a baking sheet. Chill in the fridge for at least 1 hour before serving.

COCONUT ALMOND CHOCOLATE ENERGY BALLS

Replace the walnuts with heart-healthy almonds and be sure to roll these tasty balls of energy in shredded coconut for added texture.

Calories: **72** Total fat: **5 g** Saturated fat: **1 g** Total carbohydrate: **8 g** Dietary fibre: **2 g** Sugars: **5 g** Protein: **2 g**

Ingredients

175 g (6 oz) almonds

100 g (3½ oz) pitted Medjool dates

25 g (1 oz) unsweetened cocoa powder or raw cacao powder

25 g (1 oz) shredded coconut

pinch of sea salt

1 teaspoon pure vanilla extract

2 tablespoons cacao nibs

shredded coconut, for rolling

1 Follow the instructions for the Decadent Chocolate Brownie Energy Balls (see above), leaving the cacao nibs until last – pulse the cacao nibs in for the last 10–15 seconds.

 Try This

Decadent Chocolate Brownie Energy Balls Toppings
Roll your Decadent Chocolate Brownie Energy Balls in hemp seeds, shredded coconut or cacao nibs for extra flavour and a nutritional boost (see Toppings panel, page 73).

Ingredients

175 g (6 oz) cashews (or almonds)

100 g (3½ oz) pitted Medjool dates

25 g (1 oz) unsweetened cocoa powder or raw cacao powder

pinch of sea salt

1 teaspoon pure vanilla extract

1 tablespoon grated orange zest

2 tablespoons cacao nibs

shredded coconut or orange zest, for rolling

Ingredients

100 g (3½ oz) pecans (or almonds)

100 g (3½ oz) pitted Medjool dates

½ teaspoon ground cinnamon

¼ teaspoon cayenne pepper (add in a drop more for additional spice)

3 tablespoons raw cacao or unsweetened cocoa powder

pinch of sea salt

2 tablespoons cacao nibs

chopped pecans or cocoa powder, for rolling

ZESTY ORANGE CHOCOLATE ENERGY BALLS

Add a shot of vitamin C to your chocolate energy balls with this zesty variation.

Calories: **66** Total fat: **4 g** Saturated fat: **0 g** Total carbohydrate: **7 g** Dietary fibre: **1 g** Sugars: **4 g** Protein: **2 g**

1 Follow the instructions for the Decadent Chocolate Brownie Energy Balls (see opposite), leaving the orange zest and cacao nibs until last – add the orange zest when the mixture is smooth and pulse, then blend until incorporated. Pulse the cacao nibs in for the final 10–15 seconds.

TURN UP THE HEAT CHOCOLATE ENERGY BALLS

If you enjoy a little spice with your sweet, try turning up the heat with cinnamon and cayenne added to the mix.

Calories: **63** Total fat: **5 g** Saturated fat: **0 g** Total carbohydrate: **7 g** Dietary fibre: **1 g** Sugars: **4 g** Protein: **1 g**

1 Follow the instructions for the Decadent Chocolate Brownie Energy Balls (see opposite), leaving the cacao nibs until last – pulse them in for the last 10–15 seconds.

Below: Zesty Orange Chocolate Energy Balls

HIGH-ENERGY BALLS

These bite-sized snacks are not only delicious, but they also stabilize your blood sugar in-between meals with a hefty dose of plant-based protein and healthy fats. Whip up a batch at the beginning of the week, and store in the fridge or freezer to have ready any time you need a tasty pick-me-up.

Yield: 20 2.5-cm (1-in) balls
Serving size: 1 energy ball
Prep time: 10–15 minutes, plus 1 hour chilling
Storage: Up to 3 days in an airtight container in the fridge or 1 month in the freezer

CASHEW AND CARDAMOM LIME ENERGY BALLS

Used in Ayurvedic medicine, cardamom has a whole host of health benefits. This recipe is a tasty way to sprinkle in this super-spice to your diet while enjoying its detoxifying properties.

Calories: **67** Total fat: **3 g** Saturated fat: **1 g** Total carbohydrate: **10 g** Dietary fibre: **1 g** Sugars: **7 g** Protein: **1 g**

Ingredients

175 g (6 oz) cashews

135 g (4¾ oz) pitted Medjool dates

75 g (3 oz) unsweetened shredded coconut, plus extra for rolling

1 tablespoon maple syrup

2 tablespoons lime juice

½ teaspoon pure vanilla extract

½ teaspoon sea salt

⅛ teaspoon ground cardamom

1 tablespoon grated lime zest, plus extra for rolling

1   Place the nuts in a food processor and pulse until crumbly, but not completely smooth. Add the remaining ingredients, except for the cardamom and lime zest. Process until the mixture is well combined. Add the cardamom and lime zest and pulse for about 30 seconds until all the ingredients are incorporated – the mixture will be sticky. If the mixture is too sticky to handle, place in the freezer for about 15–20 minutes, until it is firm enough to roll.

2   Use a small spoon to scoop out the mixture and roll into bite-sized morsels, shaping with slightly wet hands.

3   Mix the extra shredded coconut and lime zest together in a small bowl and use it to lightly cover each energy ball. Place them on a baking sheet and chill in the fridge for at least 1 hour before serving. Enjoy!

LEMON DROP ENERGY BALLS

Tasty, sweet and tangy all rolled into one ball. One bite and you'll understand why this is my family's favourite flavour.

Calories: **84** Total fat: **5 g** Saturated fat: **1 g** Total carbohydrate: **9 g** Dietary fibre: **2 g** Sugars: **7 g** Protein: **2 g**

Ingredients

175 g (6 oz) almonds (or cashews)

135 g (4¾ oz) pitted Medjool dates

40 g (1½ oz) unsweetened shredded coconut, plus extra for rolling

1 tablespoon maple syrup

2 tablespoons lemon juice

½ teaspoon pure vanilla extract

½ teaspoon sea salt

1 tablespoon grated lemon zest, plus extra for rolling

1   Follow the instructions for Cashew and Cardamom Lime Energy Balls (see above).

Opposite: Lemon Drop Energy Balls

Ingredients

100 g (3½ oz) walnuts

25 g (1 oz) rolled oats

1 tablespoon ground flax seeds

60 g (2½ oz) pitted Medjool dates

100 g (3½ oz) unsweetened dried apple

1 teaspoon ground cinnamon

1 tablespoon maple syrup

½ teaspoon sea salt

shredded coconut or crushed walnuts, for rolling (optional)

Ingredients

175 g (6 oz) almonds

125 g (4½ oz) unsweetened dried figs

40 g (1½ oz) unsweetened shredded coconut

1 tablespoon maple syrup

½ teaspoon pure vanilla extract

½ teaspoon sea salt

Ingredients

75 g (3 oz) macadamia nuts

75 g (3 oz) pecans

40 g (1½ oz) dried unsweetened mango (soaked, rinsed and drained)

40 g (1½ oz) dried unsweetened pineapple (soaked, rinsed and drained)

60 g (2½ oz) pitted Medjool dates

25 g (1 oz) shredded coconut, plus a little extra for rolling

1 tablespoon grated orange zest, plus extra for rolling

½ teaspoon pure vanilla extract

½ teaspoon sea salt

APPLE PIE ENERGY BALLS

Power up before a session at the gym with the taste and flavour of an apple crisp. Omega-3 rich flax seeds and walnuts make this a nutritional hit.

Calories: **63** Total fat: **4 g** Saturated fat: **0 g** Total carbohydrate: **7 g** Dietary fibre: **1 g** Sugars: **5 g** Protein: **1 g**

1 Follow the instructions for Cashew and Cardamom Lime Energy Balls (see page 126) – the walnuts need less time in the food processor though, as they can turn to powder very quickly; make certain to leave some texture.

ALMOND FIG ENERGY BALLS

Replace the dates with dried figs for a delicious fibre-filled and potassium-rich treat.

Calories: **75** Total fat: **5 g** Saturated fat: **1 g** Total carbohydrate: **7 g** Dietary fibre: **2 g** Sugars: **4 g** Protein: **2 g**

1 Follow the instructions for Cashew and Cardamom Lime Energy Balls (see page 126). The ingredients in this recipe provide a lot of texture, so the balls don't need to be rolled in anything.

TROPICAL SUNRISE ENERGY BALLS

With mango, pineapple, orange and coconut, this tropical variation will satisfy even the most stubborn sweet tooth.

Calories: **79** Total fat: **6 g** Saturated fat: **1 g** Total carbohydrate: **8 g** Dietary fibre: **1 g** Sugars: **5 g** Protein: **1 g**

1 Follow the instructions for Cashew and Cardamom Lime Energy Balls (see page 126), but soak the mango and pineapple for 10 minutes, then dry them before mixing in with the other ingredients.

NO-NUT ENERGY BITES

With the same blood-sugar balancing combination of nutrients as the High-energy Balls (see page 126), these seed-based energy bites are nourishing, tasty and packed with micronutrients. Don't let the tiny size of seeds fool you; they're a powerful source of nutrition and add protein, fibre and omega fatty acids to your diet.

Yield: 20 2.5-cm (1-in) balls
Serving size: 1 energy ball
Prep time: 15 minutes, plus 1 hour chilling
Storage: Up to 3 days in an airtight container in the fridge or up to 1 month in the freezer

Ingredients
150 g (5 oz) pumpkin seeds
100 g (3½ oz) pitted Medjool dates
50 g (2 oz) raisins
40 g (1½ oz) shredded coconut, plus extra for rolling
1 teaspoon pure vanilla extract
½ teaspoon sea salt
2 teaspoons grated fresh ginger
1 teaspoon ground cinnamon
pinch of ground cloves

GINGERBREAD ENERGY BITES

Taste the holiday season when you pop one of these energy bites in your mouth. You get bonus points for filling your body with extra ginger for muscle recovery and a nice dose of magnesium from the pumpkin seeds.

Calories: **69** Total fat: **4 g** Saturated fat: **1 g** Total carbohydrate: **8 g** Dietary fibre: **1 g** Sugars: **6 g** Protein: **2 g**

1 Place the seeds in a food processor and pulse until they are coarsely chopped but still have some texture. Add the remaining ingredients, except for the spices, and process until the mixture is well combined. Add the spices and pulse for up to 1 minute, until all the ingredients are incorporated – the mixture will be sticky.

2 With slightly wet hands, roll into 2.5-cm (1-in) balls. If the mixture is too sticky to handle, place in the freezer for about 15–20 minutes until firm enough to roll.

3 Lightly cover each energy bite with a little shredded coconut, then place them on a baking sheet.

4 Transfer the sheet to the fridge for at least 1 hour before serving. Store any remaining energy bites in an airtight container for up to 3 days in the fridge, or freeze to have on hand. Thaw for a few minutes before eating. Enjoy!

Ingredients

150 g (5 oz) sunflower seeds (almonds work well if not nut-free)

135 g (4¾ oz) pitted Medjool dates

40 g (1½ oz) shredded coconut

2 tablespoons tahini

1 tablespoon honey

½ teaspoon pure vanilla extract

½ teaspoon sea salt

sesame seeds, for rolling

Ingredients

60 g (2½ oz) pitted Medjool dates

60 g (2½ oz) dried cherries

40 g (1½ oz) hemp seeds, plus extra for rolling

40 g (1½ oz) sesame seeds, toasted

40 g (1½ oz) sunflower seeds

40 g (1½ oz) pumpkin seeds

1 teaspoon pure vanilla extract

½ teaspoon sea salt

SESAME TAHINI ENERGY BITES

Tahini, a ground paste made from sesame, has more protein than milk, plus some bone-building nutrients too. Mixed with dates, sesame seeds and honey, it creates a wonderful taste sensation.

Calories: **79** Total fat: **4 g** Saturated fat: **1 g** Total carbohydrate: **9 g** Dietary fibre: **2 g** Sugars: **7 g** Protein: **2 g**

1   Follow the instructions for the Gingerbread Energy Bites (see page 129), but roll in sesame seeds.

THREE-SEED CHERRY ENERGY BITES

In a base of sweet dried cherries, the tiny seeds come together to create a protein-packed, omega-rich energy bite.

Calories: **64** Total fat: **3 g** Saturated fat: **1 g** Total carbohydrate: **7 g** Dietary fibre: **1 g** Sugars: **5 g** Protein: **2 g**

1   Follow the basic instructions for the Gingerbread Energy Bites (see page 129), but skip the first step of processing the seeds. Place all the ingredients in the bowl of a food processor and mix together.

Right: Tahini is a paste made from ground sesame seeds. It is popularly used as an ingredient in Middle Eastern cuisine.

Opposite: Sesame Tahini Energy Bites, back; Gingerbread Energy Bites, front, page 129

NUT BUTTER BLISS BALLS

Yield: 24 1.25-cm (24½-in) balls
Serving size: 1 bliss ball
Prep time: 5–10 minutes, plus 1 hour chilling
Storage: Up to 3 days in an airtight container in the fridge, or 1 month in the freezer

Small morsels of deliciousness, these recipes have the same nutritional goodness as the other energy balls, with a bit more staying power due to the addition of healthy fat from nut butter. Perfect for activity-filled days that call for foods to sustain you for the long haul.

Ingredients

175 g (6 oz) cashews
60 g (2½ oz) cashew butter
135 g (4¾ oz) pitted Medjool dates
1 tablespoon maple syrup
½ teaspoon pure vanilla extract
½ teaspoon sea salt
crushed cashews, for rolling

SALTED CARAMEL BLISS BALLS

A simply amazing flavour – if you don't try this caramel energy ball, you'll definitely be missing out.

Calories: **65** Total fat: **3 g** Saturated fat: **1 g** Total carbohydrate: **8 g**
Dietary fibre: **1 g** Sugars: **6 g** Protein: **1 g**

1 Place the nuts in a food processor and pulse until crumbly, but not completely smooth. Add the remaining ingredients and process until the mixture is well combined.

2 Use a small spoon to scoop out the mixture and roll into 2.5-cm (1-in) morsels, using slightly wet hands.

3 Lightly cover each bliss ball with crushed cashews and place on a baking sheet. Place in the fridge for at least 1 hour before serving. Enjoy!

Ingredients

75 g (3 oz) almonds
50 g (2 oz) pecans
100 g (3½ oz) dried cranberries, cherries and goji berries (any combination)
25 g (1 oz) pitted Medjool dates
2 tablespoons almond butter
½ teaspoon pure vanilla extract
1 tablespoon maple syrup
pinch of sea salt
crushed pecans or shredded coconut, for rolling (optional)

VERY BERRY BLISS BALL

Kick your antioxidants up another notch with this combination of phytonutrient-rich cranberries, cherries and goji berries.

Calories: **66** Total fat: **4 g** Saturated fat: **0 g** Total carbohydrate: **6 g**
Dietary fibre: **1 g** Sugars: **4 g** Protein: **2 g**

1 Follow the instructions for the Salted Caramel Bliss Balls (see above).

 Cook's Note

Keep Cool
These bliss balls will get soft at room temperature due to the nut butter content. They are best eaten straight out of the fridge or freezer (allow them to thaw a bit at room temperature if eating from freezer).

Ingredients

75 g (3 oz) cashews

50 g (2 oz) walnuts

135 g (4¾ oz) pitted Medjool dates

2 tablespoons cashew butter

1 tablespoon maple syrup

1 tablespoon finely ground organic coffee

1 tablespoon raw cacao or unsweetened cocoa powder

½ teaspoon pure vanilla extract

pinch of sea salt

25 g (1 oz) shredded coconut, plus extra for rolling

Ingredients

75 g (3 oz) almonds

60 g (2½ oz) pistachios

2 tablespoons almond butter

60 g (2½ oz) dried cherries

60 g (2½ oz) pitted Medjool dates, chopped

1 tablespoon maple syrup

2 tablespoons raw cacao powder or unsweetened cocoa powder

pinch of sea salt

1 tablespoon cacao nibs

crushed pistachios or raw cacao powder or unsweetened cocoa powder, for rolling (optional)

Ingredients

100 g (3½ oz) oat flour (see Cook's Note on page 134)

40 g (1½ oz) ground flax seeds

25 g (1 oz) coconut flour

pinch of sea salt

1 teaspoon ground cinnamon

125 g (4 oz) nut or seed butter

75 ml (3 fl oz) maple syrup

2 tablespoons coconut oil, softened

40 g (1½ oz) golden raisins

rolled oats, for rolling (optional)

TIRAMISU BLISS BALLS

Roll the flavours of a classic Italian dessert into bite-size treats. Double up the energy with caffeine from the coffee and cacao.

Calories: **64** Total fat: **4 g** Saturated fat: **1 g** Total carbohydrate: **8 g** Dietary fibre: **1 g** Sugars: **5 g** Protein: **1 g**

1 Follow the instructions for the Salted Caramel Bliss Balls (see opposite).

PISTACHIO CHOCOLATE CHERRY BLISS BALLS

A concentrated source of energy, pistachios can help to reduce bad cholesterol while supporting levels of good (HDL) cholesterol in the blood.

Calories: **63** Total fat: **3 g** Saturated fat: **0 g** Total carbohydrate: **8 g** Dietary fibre: **1 g** Sugars: **4 g** Protein: **2 g**

1 Follow the instructions for the Salted Caramel Bliss Balls (see opposite), but pulse the almonds first into small chunks, then add the pistachios. Reserve the cacao nibs until after the ingredients are mixed and pulse them in at the end, or hand-mix them into the mixture before forming into balls.

OAT RAISIN BLISS BALLS

Enjoy the delicious taste of oat raisin cookie dough with the added bonus of fibre and essential nutrients from the oats and coconut flour.

Calories: **50** Total fat: **5 g** Saturated fat: **2 g** Total carbohydrate: **9 g** Dietary fibre: **2 g** Sugars: **3 g** Protein: **2 g**

1 Mix the oat flour, ground flax seeds, coconut flour and salt in a large bowl. Add the ground cinnamon, nut or seed butter, maple syrup and coconut oil, and mix well until all the ingredients are blended together (you may want to use your hands). Once the mixture is smooth and incorporated, add the raisins and mix well again.

2 Use a small spoon to scoop out the mixture and roll into about 2.5-cm (1-in) balls (or a little larger), forming with slightly wet hands. Roll each ball in some oats, if using, so they are evenly coated. Place on a tray and set in the fridge for 1 hour.

Ingredients

100 g (3½ oz) oat flour (see Cook's Note)

40 g (1½ oz) ground flax seeds

25 g (1 oz) coconut flour

pinch of sea salt

1 teaspoon pure vanilla extract

125 g (4 oz) sunflower seed butter

75 ml (3 fl oz) maple syrup

2 tablespoons coconut oil, softened

25 g (1 oz) dried blueberries

rolled oats, for rolling (optional)

BLUEBERRY OAT BLISS BALLS

For a nut-free option, try this tasty oat-based ball packed with the antioxidant goodness of blueberries and the nutty flavour (and fibre) of coconut flour.

Calories: **82** Total fat: **5 g** Saturated fat: **2 g** Total carbohydrate: **9 g**
Dietary fibre: **2 g** Sugars: **3 g** Protein: **2 g**

1   Follow the instructions for the Oat Raisin Bliss Balls (see page 133).

 Cook's Notes

DIY Oat Flour
To make your own oat flour, blend 100 g (3½ oz) rolled oats in a food processor to make 75–100 g (3–3½ oz) oat flour.

No Food Processor Required
Unlike the other energy balls, the oat-based bliss balls do not have dates and do not require a food processor.

Below: Blueberry Oat Bliss Balls

CHOCOLATE TRUFFLES

Yield: 18 1.25-cm (½-in) truffles
Serving size: 1 truffle
Prep time: 5–10 minutes, plus 30 minutes and 1 hour chilling
Storage: Up to 1 week in an airtight container in the fridge or 1 month in the freezer

Turning to chocolate isn't such a bad thing when it involves cacao. Raw cacao is a superfood that contains more antioxidant flavonoids than red wine, green tea and blueberries. So go ahead and indulge in these tiny balls of pure joy! Just make sure to savour each decadent bite.

Ingredients

3 tablespoons coconut butter

2 tablespoons coconut oil, softened

2 tablespoons maple syrup

½ teaspoon pure vanilla extract

2 tablespoons nut butter, softened (or at room temperature)

25 g (1 oz) raw cacao powder or unsweetened cocoa powder, plus extra for rolling

pinch of sea salt

DECADENT CHOCOLATE TRUFFLES

A simple and delicious dessert full of healthy fats from coconut butter and oil, plus a rich chocolate taste to keep your inner chocoholic satisfied.

Calories: **53** Total fat: **5 g** Saturated fat: **4 g** Total carbohydrate: **3 g** Dietary fibre: **1 g** Sugars: **1 g** Protein: **1 g**

1 Place the coconut butter, coconut oil, maple syrup and vanilla extract in a medium bowl and mix until smooth. Add the nut butter and stir until combined. Mix in the cacao powder and sea salt and stir well until the powder dissolves completely. Place the mixture in the fridge for 30 minutes to chill.

2 Remove from the fridge and form into small balls by hand. Roll in cacao powder and set the balls on a tray or plate before placing in the fridge to set for 1 hour. Serve these melt-in-your-mouth treats chilled.

Ingredients

3 tablespoons coconut butter

2 tablespoons coconut oil, softened

2 tablespoons maple syrup

½ teaspoon pure vanilla extract

2 tablespoons nut butter, softened (or at room temperature)

25 g (1 oz) raw cacao powder or unsweetened cocoa powder, plus extra for rolling

pinch of sea salt

½ teaspoon mint extract

1 tablespoon cacao nibs

CHOCOLATE MINT TRUFFLES

Simply swirl in your mint extract before cooling to create an elegant after-dinner truffle with none of the unwanted ingredients hidden in ready-made versions.

Calories: **53** Total fat: **5 g** Saturated fat: **4 g** Total carbohydrate: **3 g** Dietary fibre: **1 g** Sugars: **1 g** Protein: **1 g**

1 Follow the instructions for the Decadent Chocolate Truffles (see above), adding in the mint extract and cacao nibs to the smooth mixture before placing in the fridge for chilling.

Ingredients

3 tablespoons coconut butter

2 tablespoons coconut oil, softened

2 tablespoons maple syrup

½ teaspoon pure vanilla extract

2 tablespoons almond butter, softened (or at room temperature)

25 g (1 oz) raw cacao powder or unsweetened cocoa powder

pinch of sea salt

½ teaspoon almond extract

1 tablespoon crushed almonds (optional)

shredded coconut, for rolling

Ingredients

3 tablespoons coconut butter

2 tablespoons coconut oil, softened

2 tablespoons maple syrup

½ teaspoon pure vanilla extract

2 tablespoons cashew butter, softened (or at room temperature)

25 g (1 oz) raw cacao powder or unsweetened cocoa powder, plus extra for rolling

pinch of sea salt

1 teaspoon grated orange zest

shredded coconut for rolling, optional

CHOCOLATE ALMOND COCONUT TRUFFLES

Roll your chocolate and almond butter-infused truffles in coconut and enjoy a nutrient-dense, protein-packed treat.

Calories: **55** Total fat: **5 g** Saturated fat: **5 g** Total carbohydrate: **3 g** Dietary fibre: **1 g** Sugars: **1 g** Protein: **1 g**

1 Follow the instructions for the Decadent Chocolate Truffles (see page 135), adding in the almond extract and crushed almonds, if using, to the smooth mixture. Roll in the shredded coconut (instead of cacao powder) once formed into balls, before placing in the fridge for chilling.

CHOCOLATE ORANGE TRUFFLES

Packed with healthy plant-based energy from coconut, cashew butter and cacao, the grated orange zest lends a citrus freshness to this truffle.

Calories: **51** Total fat: **4 g** Saturated fat: **3 g** Total carbohydrate: **4 g** Dietary fibre: **1 g** Sugars: **2 g** Protein: **1 g**

1 Follow the instructions for the Decadent Chocolate Truffles (see page 135), adding in the orange zest to the smooth mixture. Roll in the shredded coconut or cacao powder when formed into balls, before placing in the fridge for chilling.

 Try This

Nut-free Option
Use sunflower seed butter instead of the nut butter for a nut-free variation.

Decadent Chocolate Truffles,
page 135; Chocolate Almond
Coconut Truffles, page 136

Chai-Spiced Truffles, page 138

NON-CHOCOLATE TRUFFLES

Yield: 18 1.25-cm (18½-in) truffles
Serving size: 1 truffle
Prep time: 5–10 minutes, plus 30 minutes and 1 hour chilling
Storage: Up to 1 week in an airtight container in the fridge or 1 month in the freezer

Made with the same nourishing ingredients as the chocolate truffles (minus the cacao), these ultra-smooth and sinful-tasting treats happen to work perfectly after dinner when you're craving just a bit of a little something sweet.

CHAI-SPICED TRUFFLES

Ingredients

3 tablespoons coconut butter
2 tablespoons coconut oil, softened
2 tablespoons maple syrup
½ teaspoon pure vanilla extract
2 tablespoons nut butter, softened (or at room temperature)
2 tablespoons coconut flour
pinch of sea salt
½ teaspoon ground cinnamon
¼ teaspoon ground ginger
pinch of ground nutmeg
pinch of ground cardamom
pinch of cloves
crushed almonds or unsweetened shredded coconut, for rolling (optional)

Try this melt-in-your-mouth truffle with all the flavours of a chai tea latte. Healing, warming ginger, cinnamon, nutmeg and cardamom combine in this delicious truffle.

Calories: **44** Total fat: **4 g** Saturated fat: **3 g** Total carbohydrate: **2 g** Dietary fibre: **1 g** Sugars: **0 g** Protein: **1 g**

1 Place the coconut butter, coconut oil, maple syrup and vanilla extract in a medium bowl and mix until smooth. Add the nut butter and stir until combined. Mix in the coconut flour and sea salt, and stir well until the powder dissolves completely. Add the spices and mix together. Place the mixture in the fridge for 30 minutes to chill.

2 Remove from the fridge and form into small balls using slightly wet hands. Roll in crushed almonds or shredded coconut, if using, and set the balls on a tray or plate before placing in the fridge to set for 1 hour. Serve these tempting treats chilled.

BLACK SESAME TRUFFLES

Ingredients

3 tablespoons coconut butter
2 tablespoons coconut oil, softened
1 tablespoon tahini
½ teaspoon pure vanilla extract
1 tablespoon nut butter
2 tablespoons coconut flour
pinch of sea salt
1–2 tablespoons black sesame seeds, for rolling

Add some crunch, calcium and colour to your truffles with the addition of black sesame seeds.

Calories: **48** Total fat: **5 g** Saturated fat: **3 g** Total carbohydrate: **2 g** Dietary fibre: **2 g** Sugars: **0 g** Protein: **1 g**

1 Follow the instructions for the Chai-Spiced Truffles (see above).

DESSERTS AND PARFAITS

Everyone loves a sweet treat now and then, and it is important not only to feed your body with whole foods but to also enjoy them. These desserts are delicious, decadent and good for your mind, body and soul. By avoiding refined sugars and sneaking in veggies and other nutrient-dense foods, these heavenly treats pack a nutritional punch and won't knock your blood sugar balance off.

Baked Chewy Oat
Chocolate Chip Cookies,
page 141

PROTEIN-PACKED COOKIES

Yield: 16 cookies

Serving size: 1 cookie

Prep time: 10 minutes, plus 1 hour to set

Storage: 5 days in the fridge or 1 month in the freezer

There's no need to feel guilty about putting your hand in the whole food cookie jar. One bite and you won't even miss the sugar, white flour or processed ingredients. Filled with healthy fats, protein and nutrient-dense superfoods, choose any one of these cookies as a midday pick-me-up or satisfying dessert.

GO NUTS RAW COOKIE DOUGH

Ingredients

50 g (2 oz) pecans

50 g (2 oz) walnuts

175 g (6 oz) cashews

25 g (1 oz) goji berries

1 tablespoon coconut oil

2 tablespoons maple syrup

½ teaspoon ground cinnamon

1 teaspoon pure vanilla extract

pinch of sea salt

2 tablespoons cacao nibs

While not a traditional cookie, you won't believe how much these nut- and protein-packed treats taste like raw cookie dough. Confession: I've been known to eat these for breakfast.

Calories: **124** Total fat: **9 g** Saturated fat: **2 g** Total carbohydrate: **8 g** Dietary fibre: **1 g** Sugars: **3 g** Protein: **3 g**

1 Place the pecans, walnuts and cashews in a food processor and process until the nuts are in small pieces but not a powder.

2 Add the goji berries, coconut oil, maple syrup, cinnamon, vanilla extract and salt. Combine all ingredients and process until a dough-like consistency begins to form, making sure to leave some chunks of nuts and goji berries. Add the cacao nibs and pulse a few times to incorporate.

3 Use a small scooper, about 4 cm (1½ in), or roll 1 tablespoon at a time in your hands – because the mixture is mostly nuts, it will feel oily if you roll the balls by hand. Make sure to pack the dough tightly against the scooper or in your hands before placing on a plate or tray. Flatten the bottom onto a tray to form a dome shape. Put in the freezer for 30 minutes to set.

SEEDS OF CHANGE COOKIES

Ingredients

50 g (2 oz) walnuts

75 g (3 oz) cashews

25 g (1 oz) hemp seeds

40 g (1½ oz) sunflower seeds

40 g (1½ oz) sesame seeds

25 g (1 oz) shredded coconut

2 tablespoons maple syrup

1 tablespoon coconut oil

1 teaspoon pure vanilla extract

½ teaspoon ground cinnamon

pinch of sea salt

25 g (1 oz) dried figs

Another amazing raw cookie packed full of essential minerals and vitamins from the hemp seeds, sunflower seeds and sesame seeds.

Calories: **111** Total fat: **9 g** Saturated fat: **2 g** Total carbohydrate: **6 g** Dietary fibre: **1 g** Sugars: **2 g** Protein: **3 g**

1 Follow the instructions for the Go Nuts Raw Cookie Dough (see above) by first processing the nuts in a food processor, then adding in the seeds and all other ingredients, except the dried figs. Chop the figs by hand into small pieces and mix into the cookie dough mixture before forming into cookies.

Yield: 14 cookies
Prep Time: 10 minutes, plus
12 minutes baking
Storage: 1 day at room temperature
or 1 month in the freezer

Ingredients

150 g (5 oz) almond flour
50 g (2 oz) rolled oats
½ teaspoon bicarbonate of soda
½ teaspoon sea salt
40 g (1½ oz) shredded coconut
1 egg, slightly beaten
60 ml (2 fl oz) coconut oil, softened
60 ml (2 fl oz) honey
40 g (1½ oz) chocolate chips

BAKED CHEWY OAT CHOCOLATE CHIP COOKIES

A refined-sugar-free and gluten-free cookie that tastes so good,
you won't miss a thing.

Calories: **167** Total fat: **13 g** Saturated fat: **6 g** Total carbohydrate: **12 g**
Dietary fibre: **2 g** Sugars: **8 g** Protein: **4 g**

1   Preheat the oven to 150°C (300°F).

2   Mix together the almond flour, oats, bicarbonate of soda, sea
     salt and shredded coconut in a large bowl and set aside.

3   In a separate bowl, slightly beat the egg, then add the coconut
     oil and honey. Mix together.

4   Add the wet ingredients to the bowl of dry ingredients and
     stir until smooth. Pour in the chocolate chips and mix again.

5   Use a small scooper or spoon to roll the mixture into balls,
     using about 2 teaspoons of dough. Place on a baking sheet
     and press slightly to flatten the top. Bake for about
     10–12 minutes, or until the cookies are browned around
     the edges. Allow to cool on a wire rack before serving.

Below: Go Nuts Raw Cookie Dough, page 140

MAKE-AHEAD LAYERED PARFAITS

Yield: 450 g (1 lb)
Serving size: 450 g (1 lb)
Prep time: 5–10 minutes
Storage: Best consumed immediately or can be stored in the fridge for up to 1 day

Layers and layers of DIY yogurt, chia seed pudding, crunchy granola and fresh fruit make for a delicious dessert or perfectly balanced breakfast. Whatever time of the day you enjoy your parfait, use these suggestions as inspiration to build your own, and customize these beautiful jars to meet your specific energy needs.

Try This

Energy Boost
For an energy-dense Chocolate and Vanilla Pudding Parfait, use half a jar of Banana Almond Crunch Overnight Oats (see page 71) as a base and layer with Simple Chia Seed Pudding (see page 68) and fresh banana. Top with cacao nibs for an extra kick! Save the other half of the overnight oats to enjoy as a mid-afternoon pre-workout snack, or use it in a parfait the next day.

Ingredients

125 g (4 oz) Chocolate Chia Seed Pudding (see page 70)

½ banana (or more)

125 g (4 oz) Simple Chia Seed Pudding (see page 68)

25 g (1 oz) Vanilla Maple Crunch Granola (see page 85)

cacao nibs, for topping

CHOCOLATE AND VANILLA PUDDING PARFAIT

Remember as a child how one of the toughest decisions was chocolate or vanilla? Now you don't have to pick. Enjoy both in these delicious and nutritious layers.

Calories: **319** Total fat: **14 g** Saturated fat: **4 g** Total carbohydrate: **29 g** Dietary fibre: **6 g** Sugars: **20 g** Protein: **8 g**

1   Assemble the ingredients layer by layer in a glass or a jar. If making in advance, set the granola aside until ready to eat, or place it as the top layer to prevent it from getting soggy. Have fun and switch it up each time!

Ingredients

120 ml (4 fl oz) Vanilla Cashew Yogurt (see page 159)

150 g (5 oz) blueberries

125 g (4 oz) Simple Chia Seed Pudding (see page 68)

25 g (1 oz) Buckwheat Crunchy Granola (see page 85)

BLUEBERRY STREUSEL PARFAIT

Blueberries combine beautifully with the cashew yogurt and Buckwheat Crunchy Granola (see page 85) for a sweet sensation.

Calories: **527** Total fat: **27 g** Saturated fat: **7 g** Total carbohydrate: **59 g** Dietary fibre: **9 g** Sugars: **29 g** Protein: **14 g**

1   Follow the instructions for the Chocolate and Vanilla Pudding Parfait (see above).

Ingredients

125 g (4 oz) Pumpkin Spice Chia Seed Pudding (see page 70)

25 g (1 oz) Sunflower Butter and Fig Spiced Granola (see page 87), reserving 1 tablespoon for topping

120 ml (4 fl oz) coconut yogurt

dried fruits (cranberries, apricots, goji berries, golden raisins), to top

SPICED FIG PARFAIT CRUNCH

Bonus: you get double the dose of anti-inflammatory spices from the granola and the Pumpkin Spice Chia Seed Pudding (see page 70).

Calories: **371** Total fat: **16 g** Saturated fat: **7 g** Total carbohydrate: **44 g** Dietary fibre: **5 g** Sugars: **32 g** Protein: **10 g**

1   Follow the instructions for the Chocolate and Vanilla Pudding Parfait (see above).

Ingredients

125 g (4 oz) Coconut Raspberry Chia Seed Pudding (see page 70)

150 g (5 oz) fresh mixed berries, plus extra for topping

125 g (4 oz) Zesty Lemon Chia Seed Pudding (see page 68)

1 tablespoon Cranberry Orange Quinoa Granola (see page 86), or topping of choice

BERRY DELICIOUS PARFAIT

If you've got a big day or workout planned, add in more berries or toss some additional granola on top.

Calories: **319** Total fat: **12 g** Saturated fat: **3 g** Total carbohydrate: **36 g** Dietary fibre: **8 g** Sugars: **21 g** Protein: **11 g**

1   Follow the instructions for the Chocolate and Vanilla Pudding Parfait (see above).

Opposite: Blueberry Streusel Parfait

FROZEN BANANA SANDWICHES

Yield: 2 banana sandwiches
Serving size: 1 sandwich
Prep time: 5 minutes, plus 4 hours or overnight freezing
Storage: Up to 1 month in the freezer

When I was a kid, my mum would load up our freezer with sliced bananas filled with peanut butter. I've given my childhood treat a little nutritional upgrade with superfoods and nut butters. It takes only minutes to make, and there are no rules when it comes to mixing and matching the different nut butters and nutritional boosts.

Ingredients

1 banana

2 tablespoons almond butter

1 teaspoon cacao nibs

BANANA WITH ALMOND BUTTER AND CACAO NIBS

Add some crunch with raw cacao nibs – pure chocolate taste without any sugar or processed ingredients.

Calories: **158** Total fat: **10 g** Saturated fat: **1 g** Total carbohydrate: **17 g** Dietary fibre: **3 g** Sugars: **8 g** Protein: **4 g**

1   Peel then cut 1 banana in half lengthwise and then slice it in half horizontally. Arrange the quarters on a small baking sheet or freezer-safe plate, and spread equal amounts of nut butter on the banana slices. Top with the cacao nibs, then place two banana slices together to make two 'sandwiches'.

2   Freeze at least 3-4 hours until solid. Once frozen, remove from the tray and store in the freezer in containers, or wrap individually for a grab-and-go option.

Ingredients

1 banana

2 tablespoons natural unsweetened peanut butter

1 teaspoon Almond Butter and Chocolate Granola (page 87), or any granola

BANANA WITH PEANUT BUTTER AND GRANOLA

Sprinkle in any of the whole food granolas to shake this traditional pairing up a bit (see pages 84–87).

Calories: **155** Total fat: **8 g** Saturated fat: **1 g** Total carbohydrate: **18 g** Dietary fibre: **3 g** Sugars: **8 g** Protein: **5 g**

1   Follow the instructions for the Banana with Almond Butter and Cacao Nibs (see above).

Ingredients

1 banana

2 tablespoons sunflower seed butter

1 teaspoon shredded coconut

NUT-FREE BANANA WITH SUNFLOWER AND COCONUT

Layer your banana with sunflower seed butter and coconut.

Calories: **151** Total fat: **8 g** Saturated fat: **1 g** Total carbohydrate: **18 g** Dietary fibre: **2 g** Sugars: **7 g** Protein: **4 g**

1   Follow the instructions for the Banana with Almond Butter and Cacao Nibs (see above).

Opposite: Banana with Almond Butter and Cacao Nibs

BANANA ICE CREAM

Yield: 480 ml (17 fl oz) depending on flavour

Serving size: 240 ml (8½ fl oz)

Prep time: 10 minutes

Storage: Best consumed immediately

Have you ever dreamed about soft-serve ice cream without any of the dairy, refined sugars, or saturated fat? Well here it is. This super-simple and easy-to-make 'nice cream' or 'nana ice cream' (as it is popularly known) uses potassium-rich bananas to create a naturally sweet, creamy dessert.

Ingredients

3 bananas, sliced and frozen

drop of unsweetened plant-based milk (to make blending easy)

¾ teaspoon pure vanilla extract

pinch of sea salt

toppings of your choice, optional (see Toppings panel, page 73)

SIMPLY VANILLA BANANA ICE CREAM

Enjoy the simplicity of just bananas blended to a smooth consistency with a touch of vanilla. Add toppings for a nutritional boost (see Toppings panel, page 73).

Calories: **164** Total fat: **1 g** Saturated fat: **0 g** Total carbohydrate: **41 g** Dietary fibre: **5 g** Sugars: **22 g** Protein: **2 g**

1 Blend the bananas in a food processor. Before the mixture becomes smooth it will appear chunky. Once the banana starts to become smooth, add in the milk, vanilla and salt. Continue to process. Scrape down the sides and process until the batter achieves a smooth, creamy, soft-serve texture. This could take several minutes.

2 Top with fruit, shredded coconut or nuts, or enjoy this treat plain and simple.

Ingredients

3 bananas, sliced and frozen

drop of unsweetened plant-based milk (to make blending easy)

¾ teaspoon pure vanilla extract

pinch of sea salt

1–2 tablespoons natural unsweetened peanut butter (using DIY Nut Butter, see page 160, or any nut butter)

1 tablespoon Raspberry Chia Jam (see page 107), optional

PEANUT BUTTER AND BANANA ICE CREAM

Swirl some peanut butter into your banana ice cream to experience the taste sensation of a classic combination.

Calories: **211** Total fat: **5 g** Saturated fat: **1 g** Total carbohydrate: **42 g** Dietary fibre: **5 g** Sugars: **22 g** Protein: **4 g**

1 Follow the instructions for the Simply Vanilla Banana Ice Cream (see above), adding the peanut butter with the other ingredients. After processing, enjoy as is or swirl in a tablespoon of Raspberry Chia Jam (see page 107) for a peanut butter and jelly ice cream.

Ingredients

3 bananas, sliced and frozen

drop of unsweetened plant-based milk to make blending easy

¾ teaspoon pure vanilla extract

pinch of sea salt

1 tablespoon almond butter

1 tablespoon raw cacao powder or unsweetened cocoa powder

ALMOND BUTTER AND CHOCOLATE BANANA ICE CREAM

Bananas help to protect against muscle cramps during exercise. Pack some of their goodness into your dessert with this chocolatey variation.

Calories: **223** Total fat: **5 g** Saturated fat: **1 g** Total carbohydrate: **44 g** Dietary fibre: **6 g** Sugars: **22 g** Protein: **4 g**

1 Follow the instructions for the Simply Vanilla Banana Ice Cream (see opposite), adding the almond butter and cacao with the other ingredients.

Ingredients

2 bananas, sliced and frozen

175 g (6 oz) frozen strawberries

½ teaspoon pure vanilla extract

60 ml (2 fl oz) unsweetened coconut milk, or more/less for desired thickness

pinch of sea salt

STRAWBERRIES AND CREAM BANANA ICE CREAM

Recreate the flavours of everyone's ultimate summertime combination. Bonus: Strawberries are full of fibre and nutrients, including vitamin C to boost your immunity.

Calories: **156** Total fat: **2 g** Saturated fat: **1 g** Total carbohydrate: **36 g** Dietary fibre: **5 g** Sugars: **20 g** Protein: **2 g**

1 Follow the instructions for the Simply Vanilla Banana Ice Cream (see opposite), adding the strawberries and coconut milk with the other ingredients.

Ingredients

3 bananas, sliced and frozen

drop of unsweetened plant-based milk to make blending easy

¾ teaspoon pure vanilla extract

pinch of sea salt

½ teaspoon ground cinnamon

¼ teaspoon ground cardamom

SPICED BANANA ICE CREAM

Cinnamon and cardamom are wonderful detoxifying spices that can help support your body. Add a dash in this creamy dessert for the ultimate nourishing and perfectly spiced experience.

Calories: **112** Total fat: **1 g** Saturated fat: **0 g** Total carbohydrate: **28 g** Dietary fibre: **4 g** Sugars: **15 g** Protein: **1 g**

1 Follow the instructions for the Simply Vanilla Banana Ice Cream (see opposite), adding the cinnamon and cardamom with the other ingredients.

🥄 Try This

Chocolate Spread Option
Replace the nut butter in the Almond Butter and Chocolate Banana Ice Cream with homemade Chocolate Hazelnut Butter (see page 161) to up the chocolate factor.

Creamier Strawberries and Cream Ice Cream
For a creamier ice cream, use full-fat coconut milk.

Ingredients

2 bananas, sliced and frozen

150 g (5 oz) frozen mango

½ teaspoon pure vanilla extract

drop of unsweetened plant-based milk to make blending easy

pinch of sea salt

Yield: 60 ml (2 fl oz)
Serving size: 1 tablespoon
Prep time: 5 minutes
Storage: Up to 1 week in the fridge

Ingredients

4 tablespoons coconut oil

3 tablespoons raw cacao powder or unsweetened cocoa powder

1½ tablespoons maple syrup

1 teaspoon pure vanilla extract

pinch of sea salt

MANGO BANANA ICE CREAM

For a refreshing option, add alkalizing mangoes to the mix. The colour is spectacular!

Calories: **159** Total fat: **1 g** Saturated fat: **0 g** Total carbohydrate: **41 g**
Dietary fibre: **5 g** Sugars: **27 g** Protein: **2 g**

1   Follow the instructions for the Simply Vanilla Banana Ice Cream (see page 146).

HEALTHY CHOCOLATE SAUCE

For a real treat, drizzle your favourite flavour ice cream with this easy-to-make, all-natural superfood chocolate sauce.

Calories: **109** Total fat: **10 g** Saturated fat: **16 g** Total carbohydrate: **5 g**
Dietary fibre: **1 g** Sugars: **2 g** Protein: **1 g**

1   Bring the coconut oil to liquid form by placing the jar of coconut oil in warm water.

2   Mix all the ingredients together in a small bowl until smooth. Serve the sauce lukewarm. Refrigerate in-between uses and bring to room temperature before drizzling on banana ice cream.

Opposite: Simply Vanilla Banana Ice Cream, page 146, topped with Healthy Chocolate Sauce, mixed berries, shredded coconut and freeze-dried strawberry

 Cook's Note

Ripe Bananas
While it is important to use ripe bananas (not green ones), if the bananas are too ripe, it will give the ice cream a very strong flavour. Yellow bananas with only a few brown spots are ideal.

POPSICLES AND COCONUT ICE CUBES

Yield: Makes 6 standard popsicles (using a standard-sized mould)

Serving size: 1 popsicle

Prep time: 10–20 minutes, plus 4 hours chilling

Storage: Store in the moulds in the freezer for up to 3 weeks

These gorgeous popsicles will remind you of your favourite summer memories. Without any artificial colourings, refined sugar or processed ingredients, they are even more satisfying – both physically and emotionally.

🥄 **Try This**

Mix Fruits for Watermelon Burst Popsicles
Mix and match your fruits for these popsicles – pineapple, mango, blackberries, blueberries and nectarines all work.

Ingredients

1 large kiwi, peeled, halved lengthwise and cut into 5-mm (¼-inch) slices

1 peach, diced but not peeled

75 g (3 oz) strawberries, chopped or quartered

300 g (10½ oz) puréed watermelon

pinch of sea salt

WATERMELON BURST POPSICLES

For the kid in all of us, this fruit-only, refined-sugar-free frozen treat will keep you hydrated while satisfying your sweet tooth. Feel free to mix in whatever fruits you have on hand.

Calories: **30** Total fat: **0 g** Saturated fat: **0 g** Total carbohydrate: **7 g** Dietary fibre: **1 g** Sugars: **6 g** Protein: **1 g**

1 Combine the kiwi, peach and strawberries in a bowl. Use a spoon to fill the popsicle moulds about two-thirds full with fruit, making sure to get a good combination of fruit in the individual moulds. Add more fruit if necessary.

2 Add a pinch of salt to the watermelon purée and pour into the moulds to cover the fruit so that the moulds are a little over three-quarters full.

3 Place in the freezer for 40 minutes, then insert popsicle sticks (if the moulds have tops, ignore this step). Return to the freezer for at least 4 hours before serving.

4 Run warm water on the outside of the popsicle moulds until the popsicles can be easily removed.

Ingredients

10 g (½ oz) fresh mint leaves

120 ml (4 fl oz) boiling water

2 tablespoons honey

360 ml (12½ fl oz) grapefruit juice

pinch of sea salt

GRAPEFRUIT MINT POPSICLES

When you come in the door drenched from hot yoga, these citrus pops will be screaming your name. Grapefruit delivers a mega dose of vitamin C, while mint is cooling.

Calories: **46** Total fat: **0 g** Saturated fat: **0 g** Total carbohydrate: **11 g** Dietary fibre: **0 g** Sugars: **5 g** Protein: **0 g**

1 Place half the mint leaves in a small heat-proof bowl and pour the boiling water over the leaves. Let steep for 5 minutes, then let the mixture cool for 5 minutes.

2 Discard the mint leaves, add the honey to the soaking liquid and stir well. Pour the honey/water mixture, the grapefruit juice and a pinch of sea salt into a liquidizer. Add the remaining fresh mint leaves and blend for 15–30 seconds, until the mint is in visible flecks but not entirely smooth.

3 Pour the mixture into 6 popsicle moulds, filling a little more than three-quarters of the way. Place in the freezer for 1 hour before inserting popsicle sticks (if the moulds have tops, then ignore this step). Freeze for 4 hours total before serving.

4 Run warm water on the outside of the popsicle moulds until the popsicles can be easily removed.

Opposite: Watermelon Burst Popsicles

Ingredients

150 g (5 oz) blueberries

3 tablespoons maple syrup

1 tablespoon water

2 tablespoons lime juice

1 x 425-ml (15-oz) tin full-fat coconut milk

pinch of sea salt

BLUEBERRY COCONUT POPSICLES

A creamy melt-in-your-mouth sensation without any dairy. Blueberries can help fight the signs of aging skin – I sneak them in wherever I can.

Calories: **161** Total fat: **12 g** Saturated fat: **11 g** Total carbohydrate: **13 g**
Dietary fibre: **1 g** Sugars: **9 g** Protein: **0 g**

1   Combine the blueberries, 1 tablespoon of the maple syrup, 1 tablespoon of the lime juice and water in a small saucepan. Bring to a boil and heat until the liquid begins to thicken. Remove from the heat, and let stand for 10–15 minutes until cool. Leave blueberries whole.

2   Place the coconut milk, 2 tablespoons of the maple syrup, 1 tablespoon of the lime juice and a pinch of sea salt in a medium bowl and mix well. Pour the mixture into 6 popsicle moulds, filling about two-thirds full. Freeze for 15 minutes.

3   Once the 15 minutes have passed, add the blueberry mixture to the coconut in the popsicle moulds – some of the blueberry mixture will seep to the bottom.

4   Return to the freezer for 40 minutes before inserting a popsicle stick (if the moulds have tops, then ignore this step). Freeze for at least 4 hours total before serving.

5   Run warm water on the outside of the moulds until the popsicles can be easily removed.

Yield: 20 ice cubes
Serving size: 1 ice cube
Prep time: 5 minutes, 3 hours chill time

Ingredients

coconut water

COCONUT ICE CUBES

Drop a few of these flavourful and hydrating ice cubes into your smoothies whenever you could use an extra dose of electrolytes.

Calories: **6** Total fat: **0 g** Saturated fat: **0 g** Total carbohydrate: **2 g**
Dietary fibre: **0 g** Sugars: **1 g** Protein: **0 g**

1   Fill an ice cube tray with unsweetened coconut water to about three-quarters full. Trays vary in capacity, so you may get slightly more or fewer cubes depending on your tray. Put in the freezer for at least 4 hours before using.

2   Add to smoothies (see Slushy Smoothies, see page 44) or to the DIY Electrolyte Drinks (see page 56) for an extra boost in hydration.

🥄 **Try This**

Extra Blueberries for Blueberry Coconut Popsicles
Try adding extra blueberries to each mould before filling with coconut milk for more of a blueberry flavour.

DECADENT CHOCOLATE MOUSSE

Enjoying pleasurable foods, including dessert, is a key factor in ensuring success in your long-term healthy lifestyle. It's a bonus when that dessert includes nutrient-rich and wholesome ingredients.

Yield: About 125 g (4 oz)

Serving size: 60 g (2½ oz)

Prep time: 5 minutes, plus 1 hour to set

Storage: Up to 1 day in the fridge

Ingredients

1 ripe avocado, peeled and pitted

25 g (1 oz) raw cacao powder or unsweetened cocoa powder

3 tablespoons maple syrup (plus an extra tablespoon for a sweeter flavour, if desired)

¾ teaspoon pure vanilla extract

pinch of sea salt

1–2 tablespoons unsweetened coconut or almond milk (start with less and adjust to desired consistency)

optional toppings: shredded coconut, fresh berries, banana slices, cacao nibs, sprinkle of ground cinnamon

DECADENT CHOCOLATE MOUSSE

Have your greens and your chocolate, too, with this nourishing yet decadent chocolate mousse.

Calories: **268** Total fat: **14 g** Saturated fat: **3 g** Total carbohydrate: **35 g** Dietary fibre: **11 g** Sugars: **12 g** Protein: **5 g**

1   Place the avocado in a food processor or high-speed liquidizer and process until smooth. Add the remaining ingredients, except the milk, and blend until combined. Slowly add a splash or two of coconut or almond milk until the mixture reaches a completely smooth consistency – this is a thick dessert.

2   Transfer to a bowl and put in the fridge for at least 1 hour to set before serving. Serve in individual small bowls or glasses and add toppings of choice. Enjoy!

> ### 🥄 Try This
>
> **Turn up the Heat**
> Add in up to 1 teaspoon of cinnamon and a pinch of cayenne pepper to your Decadent Chocolate Mousse for a kick in flavour.

Right: Decadent Chocolate Mousse, topped with raspberries, cacao nibs and coconut flakes

CHOCOLATE BARK

Yield: 225 g (8 oz)

Serving size: 25 g (1 oz)

Prep time: 20 minutes, plus
30 minutes chilling

Storage: Up to 4 days in the fridge,
or freeze for up to 1 month

I have to warn you: once you've made a batch of my homemade
chocolate bark, you might have to put a lock on your fridge
for some portion control. A simple recipe for a deliciously
decadent sweet that is free from refined sugars and full of
antioxidants and healthy fats.

Ingredients

120 ml (4 fl oz) cacao butter

60 g (2½ oz) raw cacao powder or unsweetened cocoa powder

3 tablespoons maple syrup

½ teaspoon pure vanilla extract

pinch of sea salt

1 tablespoon hemp seeds

2 tablespoons goji berries

2 tablespoons mulberries

SUPERFOOD SEEDED CHOCOLATE BARK

Raw cacao, goji berries and mulberries equal superfoods galore. Sprinkle on some hemp seeds for a touch of nourishing micronutrients and protein.

Calories: **191** Total fat: **15 g** Saturated fat: **8 g** Total carbohydrate: **13 g**
Dietary fibre: **2 g** Sugars: **6 g** Protein: **2 g**

1 Line a small tray or plate with baking paper and set in the fridge. Place the hemp seeds, goji berries and mulberries in a small bowl and set aside.

2 Melt the cacao butter in a double boiler or a heatproof bowl set over a small saucepan with a few inches of simmering water. Stir the cacao butter continuously until it begins to melt – this process can take several minutes (do not boil the cacao butter). Once melted, remove from the heat and allow to cool to a warm temperature. Add the cacao powder, maple syrup, vanilla extract and sea salt. Mix until smooth.

3 Pour the mixture onto the tray and allow to cool for 2 minutes, then sprinkle with the seeds and berries.

4 Place the bark in the freezer for 30 minutes, before breaking it up into individual pieces.

Ingredients

120 ml (4 fl oz) cacao butter

60 g (2½ oz) raw cacao powder or unsweetened cocoa powder

3 tablespoons maple syrup

½ teaspoon pure vanilla extract

pinch of sea salt

2 tablespoons pistachios, roughly chopped

25 g (1 oz) dried cherries, roughly chopped

PISTACHIO AND CHERRY CHOCOLATE BARK

The richness of the cacao, the saltiness of the pistachios and the sweetness of cherries in this bark variation makes for a mouth-watering, winning mix.

Calories: **189** Total fat: **16 g** Saturated fat: **9 g** Total carbohydrate: **13 g**
Dietary fibre: **2 g** Sugars: **5 g** Protein: **2 g**

1 Follow the instructions for the Superfood Seeded Chocolate Bark (see above).

Cook's Note

Careful Storage
This handmade chocolate is delicate and will melt at room temperature.

Opposite: Pistachio and Cherry Chocolate Bark

Ingredients

120 ml (4 fl oz) cacao butter

60 g (2½ oz) raw cacao powder or unsweetened cocoa powder

3 tablespoons maple syrup

½ teaspoon pure vanilla extract

pinch of sea salt

25 g (1 oz) sliced almonds

1 tablespoon cacao nibs

⅓ teaspoon Himalayan sea salt

ALMONDS, CACAO NIBS AND HIMALAYAN SEA SALT CHOCOLATE BARK

A great nourishing recipe to support your body, this classic combination provides antioxidants from the cacao and protein from almonds. The added Himalayan sea salt seals the deal.

Calories: **189** Total fat: **16 g** Saturated fat: **9 g** Total carbohydrate: **10 g**
Dietary fibre: **2 g** Sugars: **3 g** Protein: **2 g**

1 Follow the instructions for the Superfood Seeded Chocolate Bark (see page 155).

Ingredients

120 ml (4 fl oz) melted cacao butter

60 g (2½ oz) raw cacao powder or unsweetened cocoa powder

3 tablespoons maple syrup

½ teaspoon pure vanilla extract

pinch of sea salt

40 g (1½ oz) dried blueberries (roughly chop if they are particularly plump)

2 tablespoons coconut flakes

BLUEBERRY AND COCONUT CHOCOLATE BARK

Almost too pretty to eat, this variation combines the nutritional goodness of blueberries with the good fats from the coconut flakes.

Calories: **183** Total fat: **15 g** Saturated fat: **9 g** Total carbohydrate: **12 g**
Dietary fibre: **2 g** Sugars: **5 g** Protein: **1 g**

1 Follow the instructions for the Superfood Seeded Chocolate Bark (see page 155).

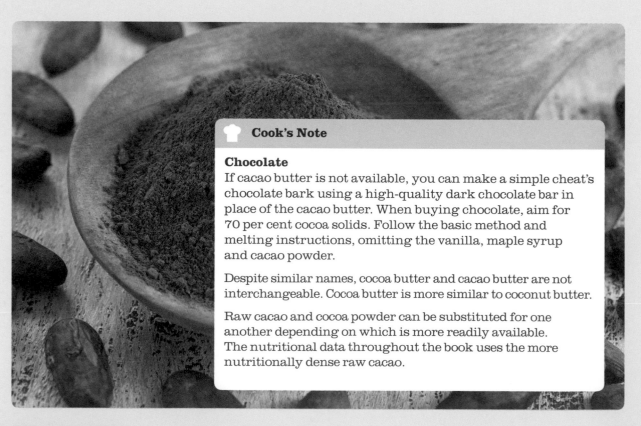

🍴 Cook's Note

Chocolate

If cacao butter is not available, you can make a simple cheat's chocolate bark using a high-quality dark chocolate bar in place of the cacao butter. When buying chocolate, aim for 70 per cent cocoa solids. Follow the basic method and melting instructions, omitting the vanilla, maple syrup and cacao powder.

Despite similar names, cocoa butter and cacao butter are not interchangeable. Cocoa butter is more similar to coconut butter.

Raw cacao and cocoa powder can be substituted for one another depending on which is more readily available. The nutritional data throughout the book uses the more nutritionally dense raw cacao.

WHOLE FOOD STAPLES

These recipes are the building blocks for your whole food kitchen. Plant-based milks, nut butters and coconut yogurt are all excellent choices for vegans and people with lactose intolerance. When you have a batch of your favourite nut milk and nut butter on standby, you'll always be set to whip up some chia seed pudding, blend yourself a balanced smoothie or throw together a batch of energy balls. The only hard part will be deciding which recipe to make.

DIY YOGURT

Yield: See each recipe
Serving size: 100 g (3½ oz), unless otherwise noted
Prep time: See each recipe
Storage: See each recipe

Fermented foods and probiotics are an important addition to any diet. The good bacteria helps to support gut health, build immunity and reduce inflammation in the body. These plant-based yogurts can also add creaminess to other whole food snacks.

Yield: 860 g (1 lb 14 oz)
Prep time: 10 minutes to prepare, plus 2½ days (or more) to ferment
Storage: Up to 1 week in the fridge

Ingredients
2 x 425-ml (15-oz) tins full-fat unsweetened coconut milk

2 tablespoons lemon juice

1 tablespoon honey

pinch of sea salt

1 teaspoon pure vanilla extract (optional)

½ teaspoon probiotic powder (or 2 probiotic capsules)

GO NUTS FOR COCONUT YOGURT

By using coconut milk and probiotic powder, you can quickly create a tasty, gut-supporting yogurt in your very own kitchen.

Calories: **231** Total fat: **23 g** Saturated fat: **0 g** Total carbohydrate: **8 g**
Dietary fibre: **0 g** Sugars: **4 g** Protein: **2 g**

1   Open the tins of coconut milk and place the solidified part of the milk into a liquidizer. Add the watery coconut liquid from 1 tin (see Cook's Note below). Mix in the lemon juice, honey, salt, vanilla extract (if using) and probiotic powder (if using capsules, open contents into the liquidizer). Blend for 1–2 minutes, until all the ingredients are well combined.

2   Transfer the mixture into a wide-mouthed 1-litre jar (mason jars work well). Allow the coconut milk to culture at room temperature, with the top slightly ajar, for 48 hours (less time in warm temperatures). Place the jar in the fridge for a further 12 hours before eating.

3   For a thicker consistency, wait 1 more day (4 days total) for the yogurt to resemble a Greek yogurt consistency. Open the jar, mix well, and enjoy your homemade yogurt.

 Cook's Notes

Cool Coconut Milk
In warmer climates, the liquid and fat in coconut milk tins will not separate. Chill the tins before opening to ensure separation.

Probiotics
Probiotics are widely available and can be purchased at any natural food store in powdered or capsule form. If using a capsule, simply open it up and release the powder into your DIY yogurt or smoothies. Make sure that the probiotic has adequate numbers of live bacteria to support digestive health, including the two most important groups: *Lactobacilli* and *Bifidobacteria*.

Yield: 530 g (1 lb 2 oz)
Prep time: 10 minutes, plus 2 days
to ferment
Storage: Up to 4 days in the fridge

Ingredients

250 g (9 oz) cashews, soaked for
  2–4 hours, drained, then rinsed
  (see Cook's Note, page 103)

240 ml (8½ fl oz) filtered water

¼ teaspoon probiotic powder
  (1 probiotic capsule)

2 teaspoons pure vanilla extract

1 tablespoon honey

pinch of sea salt

VANILLA CASHEW YOGURT

Cashews make a naturally sweet, creamy base for a non-dairy
yogurt, so you can enjoy gut-healing benefits along with the
addition of plant-based protein from the cashews.

Calories: **210** Total fat: **14 g** Saturated fat: **2 g** Total carbohydrate: **14 g**
Dietary fibre: **1 g** Sugars: **6 g** Protein: **6 g**

1   Place all the ingredients in a liquidizer and blend for
    2–4 minutes, or until smooth. Stop to scrape down the
    sides of the liquidizer halfway through.

2   Place the mixture in a wide-mouthed 1-litre glass jar. Store in
    a cool dark space with the lid slightly ajar for 24–48 hours.
    Stir the contents and put in the fridge – it will thicken as it
    chills. Once chilled, the yogurt is ready to eat.

Yield: 320 g (11 oz)
Serving size: 2 tablespoons
Prep time: 10 minutes, plus
4–6 hours soaking
Storage: Up to 3 days in the fridge

Ingredients

175 g (6 oz) cashews

120 ml (4 fl oz) water (plus
  additional water for soaking)

2 tablespoons maple syrup

1 teaspoon pure vanilla extract

pinch of sea salt

EASY VANILLA CASHEW CREAM

This delicious cream is thicker than a yogurt and is a flavourful
and decadent accent to use on top of fruits, chia seed pudding, a
chocolate mousse or as a layer in a parfait.

Calories: **63** Total fat: **4 g** Saturated fat: **1 g** Total carbohydrate: **5 g**
Dietary fibre: **0 g** Sugars: **2 g** Protein: **2 g**

1   Soak the cashews for 4–6 hours in a bowl with just enough
    water to cover. Drain the liquid and rinse with fresh water.

2   Place all the ingredients in a high-speed liquidizer and blend
    for 2–3 minutes to create a smooth and creamy consistency.

Ingredients

175 g (6 oz) cashews

120 ml (4 fl oz) water (plus
  additional water for soaking)

2 tablespoons maple syrup

1 teaspoon pure vanilla extract

pinch of sea salt

1–2 tablespoons lemon juice

2 teaspoons grated lemon zest

LEMONY CASHEW CREAM

The same delicious and wholesome ingredients as the Easy
Vanilla Cashew Cream, with just a little zest added to the mix.

Calories: **63** Total fat: **4 g** Saturated fat: **1 g** Total carbohydrate: **5 g**
Dietary fibre: **0 g** Sugars: **2 g** Protein: **2 g**

1   Follow the recipe for Easy Vanilla Cashew Cream (see above),
    adding in the lemon zest and juice with other ingredients.

🥄 **Try This**

Make a Thicker Yogurt
To make a thicker yogurt, leave out up to 120 ml (4 fl oz) of
the coconut liquid and save it to use in smoothies instead.

DIY NUT BUTTER

Yield: 240 g (8½ oz)
Serving size: 1 tablespoon
Prep time: 10–15 minutes
Storage: Up to 10 days in the fridge

Aside from being portable and delicious, nuts and seeds are nutrient-dense and filled with healthy fat, fibre and protein to provide a steady flow of energy throughout the day. Use DIY nut butters in stuffed dates, blended into smoothies or overnight oats, mixed into energy bars and balls, or by itself.

Ingredients
350 g (12 oz) nuts
pinch sea salt
1 tablespoon olive or coconut oil (optional)

BASIC NUT BUTTER

Start with the basics, and then I challenge you to play around with different nuts and seeds, spices, and flavour combinations.

Calories: **80** Total fat: **7 g** Saturated fat: **1 g** Total carbohydrate: **3 g**
Dietary fibre: **2 g** Sugars: **1 g** Protein: **3 g**

1   Place the nuts and salt in a food processor and process for about 5 minutes, making sure to scrape down the sides. The nuts will go from a crumbly consistency to a smoother one. Continue to process the nuts until they resemble a nut butter. This may take up to 10 minutes.

2   For a creamier consistency, add a tablespoon of olive oil or coconut oil. Store in a dark place or in the fridge for 10 days.

Ingredients
350 g (12 oz) almonds
4 pitted Medjool dates
1 teaspoon sea salt
1 tablespoon olive or coconut oil (optional)

SALTED CARAMEL ALMOND BUTTER

The name alone says it all. I have to hide this creamy, sweet and salty nut butter from myself. Don't say I didn't warn you!

Calories: **120** Total fat: **9 g** Saturated fat: **1 g** Total carbohydrate: **8 g**
Dietary fibre: **3 g** Sugars: **5 g** Protein: **4 g**

1   Follow the instructions for the Basic Nut Butter (see above), adding the almonds and dates to the food processor and processing until the mixture has a creamy consistency.

Ingredients
350 g (12 oz) cashews (can use roasted unsalted)
½ teaspoon sea salt
½ teaspoon ground cinnamon
1 tablespoon olive or coconut oil (optional)

CINNAMON CASHEW BUTTER

Double up on blood-sugar-stabilizing ingredients with cinnamon added to the cashew mix.

Calories: **80** Total fat: **7 g** Saturated fat: **1 g** Total carbohydrate: **4 g**
Dietary fibre: **1 g** Sugars: **1 g** Protein: **3 g**

1   Follow the instructions for the Basic Nut Butter (see above), adding the cashews to the food processor and processing until the mixture has a creamy consistency. Add the cinnamon for the last 1–2 minutes of processing.

Yield: 300 g (10½ oz)
Serving size: 1 tablespoon
Prep time: 20 minutes
Storage: Up to 1 week in the fridge

Ingredients

250 g (9 oz) hazelnuts

3 tablespoons cocoa or raw cacao powder

1 teaspoon pure vanilla extract

3 tablespoons maple syrup

1 tablespoon coconut oil, melted

pinch of sea salt

CHOCOLATE HAZELNUT BUTTER

Good enough to eat by the spoonful, you'll get a mouthful of antioxidants from the cacao and heart-healthy nutrients from hazelnuts.

Calories: **94** Total fat: **9 g** Saturated fat: **1 g** Total carbohydrate: **3 g** Dietary fibre: **1 g** Sugars: **2 g** Protein: **2 g**

1 Preheat the oven to 200°C (400°F). Roast the hazelnuts on a baking sheet for about 6–8 minutes. Remove from the oven and allow to cool.

2 Use a paper towel to hold the hazelnuts and rub gently to easily remove the skin – don't worry if it doesn't come off completely.

3 Place the hazelnuts in a food processor and process until you have a smooth texture.

4 Add the cacao powder, vanilla extract, maple syrup, and coconut oil, and blend. Add the sea salt for the last 2 minutes of the process. If the mixture is too thick, add a few tablespoons of plant-based milk.

Ingredients

200 g (7 oz) walnuts

pinch sea salt

1 tablespoon maple syrup

1 teaspoon pure vanilla extract

VANILLA MAPLE WALNUT BUTTER

Walnuts turn extra creamy in less time than the other nuts. We use the whole nut in this recipe, giving you all the benefits of the phenol-rich skin.

Calories: **100** Total fat: **10 g** Saturated fat: **1 g** Total carbohydrate: **3 g** Dietary fibre: **1 g** Sugars: **1 g** Protein: **2 g**

1 Blend the walnuts and salt in a food processor for about 5 minutes. Once the nuts become smooth, add the maple syrup and vanilla extract and process for another 2–3 minutes.

 Cook's Notes

Creamier Consistency
For a creamier consistency in Chocolate Hazelnut Butter, pulse in a few tablespoons of nut milk (see page 162) to thin it out. The nut butter will have a shorter shelf life, but that may not be an issue because it tastes so good.

Processing Nut Butter
Be a little patient with your food processor, as it takes time for the nuts to transform from their whole state into a creamy and spreadable form.

Keep an eye on walnuts when blending, as they process faster than other nuts.

SUNFLOWER SEED BUTTER

Ingredients

150 g (5 oz) sunflower seeds

1 teaspoon sea salt

1 tablespoon olive oil

1 tablespoon honey

A flavourful stand-in for nuts, sunflower seeds are high in energy and protein and taste incredible in this smooth butter.

Calories: **61** Total fat: **5 g** Saturated fat: **1 g** Total carbohydrate: **3 g** Dietary fibre: **1 g** Sugars: **1 g** Protein: **2 g**

1 Toast the seeds in a dry, medium-sized frying pan for 1–2 minutes. Watch carefully, as they can burn easily. Allow to cool.

2 Place the seeds and salt in a food processor and process for at least 10 minutes, scraping down the sides. Once the seeds become creamy and resemble a peanut butter, add the olive oil, honey and salt, and process again until the mixture becomes smooth. Enjoy!

NUT MILK

Yield: 960 ml (1¾ pt), unless otherwise noted

Serving size: 240 ml (8½ fl oz)

Prep time: 5–10 minutes, plus soaking time

Storage: Up to 3 days in the fridge

Note: Strawberry Almond Milk and Hemp Seed Milk should be eaten within 2 days

Once you make your own nut milk, you'll wonder why it took you so long to jump on the DIY bandwagon. All you need are a few ingredients, a liquidizer and a nut milk bag to whip up a homemade version of this kitchen staple.

BASIC NUT MILK

Ingredients

about 150 g (5 oz) depending on the type of nuts

840–960 ml (1½–1¾ pt) filtered water

pinch of sea salt

2–3 pitted Medjool dates (or 2 tablespoons maple syrup or honey, optional)

vanilla bean or pure vanilla extract (optional)

Start with this basic recipe, and then try using different nuts, seeds, spices and flavourings. Have fun creating variations!

Calories: **252** Total fat: **18 g** Saturated fat: **1 g** Total carbohydrate: **17 g** Dietary fibre: **5 g** Sugars: **10 g** Protein: **8 g**

1 Soak the nuts for at least 6 hours or overnight in a bowl with enough water to cover. Cashews need only 4–6 hours. Drain the water and rinse the nuts.

2 Place the soaked nuts in a high-speed liquidizer with the filtered water and blend for 2–3 minutes, or until fully liquefied. Toss in a pinch of salt.

3 For a touch of sweetness, add the dates and vanilla, if using, and blend again until smooth.

4 Pour mixture into a nut milk bag set over a wide, large bowl, and squeeze out all the liquid. Discard the pulp (or save to make crackers, see page 92) and place the milk in a mason jar or airtight container. Store in the fridge for up to 3 days.

Strawberry Almond Milk, page 165

Ingredients

125 g (4 oz) Brazil nuts, soaked

840–960 ml (1½–1¾ pt) filtered water

1 teaspoon ground cinnamon

¼ teaspoon ground nutmeg

¼ teaspoon ground cardamom

3–4 pitted Medjool dates (or 2 tablespoons maple syrup)

1 teaspoon pure vanilla extract

pinch of sea salt

Ingredients

125 g (4 oz) hazelnuts

960 ml (1¾ pt) filtered water

2–3 tablespoons raw cacao powder or unsweetened cocoa powder

2 tablespoons maple syrup

1 teaspoon pure vanilla extract

pinch of sea salt

Yield: 1.5 l (2½ pt)

Ingredients

125 g (4 oz) hemp seeds

720–960 ml (1¼–1¾ pt) filtered water

pinch of sea salt

2–3 pitted Medjool dates (or 2 tablespoons maple syrup or honey, optional)

SPICED BRAZIL NUT MILK

Brazil nuts are the richest natural source of the mineral selenium, an essential antioxidant.

Calories: **258** Total fat: **19 g** Saturated fat: **4 g** Total carbohydrate: **17 g** Dietary fibre: **3 g** Sugars: **13 g** Protein: **4 g**

1   Follow the instructions for the Basic Nut Milk (see page 162), but once strained, rinse the liquidizer, then place the nut milk, spices, dates, vanilla extract and salt back in the liquidizer and blend for 1 minute.

HAZELNUT AND CHOCOLATE MILK

A grown-up version of chocolate milk with extra nutritional benefits.

Calories: **252** Total fat: **22 g** Saturated fat: **3 g** Total carbohydrate: **13 g** Dietary fibre: **4 g** Sugars: **8 g** Protein: **6 g**

1   Follow the instructions for Basic Nut Milk (see page 162), but once strained, rinse the liquidizer, then place the nut milk, raw cacao, maple syrup, vanilla extract and salt back in the liquidizer and blend for 1 minute.

HEMP SEED MILK

For a nut-free milk, try using powerful hemp seeds. Not only are they a complete protein, but you also get a mega serving of essential fatty acids including omega-3, -6 and GLA.

Calories: **260** Total fat: **19 g** Saturated fat: **1 g** Total carbohydrate: **11 g** Dietary fibre: **2 g** Sugars: **8 g** Protein: **13 g**

1   Blend the hemp seeds and filtered water in a high-speed liquidizer for 2–3 minutes, or until fully liquefied. Toss in a pinch of salt. For a touch of sweetness, add the dates, if using, and blend again until smooth.

2   Using a wide glass bowl, pour the mixture into a nut milk bag and squeeze out all the liquid. Discard the pulp (or save to make crackers, see page 92) and place the milk in a mason jar or airtight glass container.

 Cook's Note

Seed Milk
When making hemp seed milk, it is not necessary to soak the seeds.

Ingredients

175 g (6 oz) cashews

840–960 ml (1½–1¾ pt) filtered water

1 teaspoon vanilla beans, scraped (or pure vanilla extract for a more subtle flavour)

2 tablespoons maple syrup (or 2 pitted Medjool dates)

pinch of sea salt

VANILLA BEAN CASHEW MILK

A natural sweetener, vanilla lends an incredible richness to this milk. Using the whole bean will elevate the taste and intensity of your milk.

Calories: **264** Total fat: **19 g** Saturated fat: **3 g** Total carbohydrate: **19 g** Dietary fibre: **2 g** Sugars: **8 g** Protein: **8 g**

1   Follow the instructions for Basic Nut Milk (see page 162), but once strained, rinse the liquidizer, then place the nut milk, vanilla bean powder, maple syrup and salt back in the liquidizer and blend for 1 minute until smooth. Serve hot or cold.

Yield: 1.5 l (2½ pt)

Ingredients

175 g (6 oz) almonds

840–960 ml (1½–1¾ pt) filtered water

1 teaspoon pure vanilla extract

300 g (10½ oz) strawberries (fresh or thawed frozen)

2 pitted Medjool dates (or 2 tablespoons maple syrup or honey)

pinch of sea salt

STRAWBERRY ALMOND MILK

Reminiscent of a milkshake, this energizing milk packs in the goodness of sweet strawberries – an incredible source of vitamin C – to counter inflammation in the body.

Calories: **203** Total fat: **14 g** Saturated fat: **1 g** Total carbohydrate: **16 g** Dietary fibre: **5 g** Sugars: **9 g** Protein: **6 g**

1   Follow the instructions for Basic Nut Milk (see page 162), but once strained, rinse the liquidizer, then place the nut milk, vanilla extract, strawberries, dates and salt back in the liquidizer and blend until velvety smooth. Pour the mixture back in the nut milk bag and squeeze out all the liquid.

Ingredients

175 g (6 oz) cashews, soaked

840–960 ml (1½–1¾ pt) water

3 tablespoons fresh turmeric, sliced (or 3 teaspoons ground)

2 tablespoons grated fresh ginger (or 2 teaspoons ground)

1 teaspoon pure vanilla extract

pinch of sea salt

2 pitted dates (or 2 tablespoons maple syrup)

TURMERIC–GINGER CASHEW MILK

With the healing spices ginger and turmeric, it's hard not to feel lifted after one sip of this glass of goodness.

Calories: **278** Total fat: **19 g** Saturated fat: **3 g** Total carbohydrate: **23 g** Dietary fibre: **2 g** Sugars: **10 g** Protein: **8 g**

1   Follow the instructions for Basic Nut Milk (see page 162), but once strained, rinse the liquidizer, then place the nut milk, turmeric, ginger, vanilla extract, salt and dates back in the liquidizer and blend for 1–2 minutes until smooth. Run through the nut milk bag and discard the root pulp.

 Cook's Note

Using DIY Nut Butters and Nut Milks
The recipes in this book work really well with homemade nut milks and nut butters. If using ready-made products, always choose unsweetened varieties.

PART THREE: NUTRITIONAL INFORMATION

CHOOSING A RECIPE

There are tons of mouth-watering and nutritionally-dense recipes for you to choose from in this book. To help you find foods to meet particular demands, we have also provided nutritional information so that you can match a recipe to your individual energy needs. As well as using the colour-coding, nutritional information and tags provided for each recipe (see pages 8–9), you can also use the indexes and charts over the next few pages as quick-reference guides to finding foods to support your lifestyle.

THREE WAYS TO FIND THE BEST RECIPE FOR YOU

In this chapter there are a number of charts and indexes designed to help you determine which recipes are best suited to meet your body's energy needs.

1 Top 5 Recipes for Essential Nutrients (see pages 170–171)

In addition to fat, carbohydrate, fibre and protein, there are many other essential nutrients that your body needs in order to perform at its very best. Use this index to help you find the top five recipes for seven of the key nutrients that help to support an active lifestyle.

2 Index of Recipes by Nutritional Tag (see pages 172–173)

Throughout this book each recipe section is tagged for specific nutritional benefits so that you can quickly identify foods that will provide fast-release energy, give you a dose of calcium or help your muscles to recover after a workout, for example. Pages 172–173 list the recipes under each tag to help you get started.

3 General Index (see pages 174–176)

There are useful tips and notes throughout the book which may be helpful when you are preparing your whole food recipes. If you have a particular question about preparation methods or ingredients, turn to pages 174–176 to easily find the information you need. You can also look up recipes by food groupings in this index.

STANDARD NUTRITIONAL INFORMATION

The nutritional information in this book is based on the daily value recommendations in the author's home, the United States. For each recipe you will find simplified nutritional information, listing how much of each key nutrient one serving provides.

The chart opposite shows the total Daily Values (DV) as recommended by the U.S. Food and Drug Administration (FDA). These values are generally recommended in this book as guidelines for adults and children over four years of age around the world. This information is designed as a rough guide to nutrient intake, and your specific nutritional needs is determined by factors such as your level of physical activity, gender, age, weight and genes. Use nutritional information as a useful guide, but always be sure to listen to your body, and talk to your doctor.

RECOMMENDED DAILY VALUES FOR ADULTS*

FOOD COMPONENT	DAILY VALUE	FOOD COMPONENT	DAILY VALUE
Total Fat	65 grams (g)	Riboflavin	1.7 mg
Saturated Fat	20 g	Niacin	20 mg
Cholesterol	300 milligrams (mg)	Vitamin B6	2 mg
Sodium	2,400 mg	Folate	400 µg
Potassium	3,500 mg	Vitamin B12	6 µg
Total Carbohydrate	300 g	Biotin	300 µg
Dietary Fibre	25 g	Pantothentic acid	10 mg
Protein	50 g	Phosphorus	1,000 mg
Vitamin A	5,000 International Units (IU)	Iodine	150 µg
Vitamin C	60 mg	Magnesium	400 mg
Calcium	1,000 mg	Zinc	15 mg
Iron	18 mg	Selenium	70 µg
Vitamin D	400 IU	Copper	2 mg
Vitamin E	30 IU	Manganese	2 mg
Vitamin K	80 micrograms (µg)	Chromium	120 µg
Thiamin	1.5 mg	Molybdenum	75 µg
		Chloride	3,400 mg

This chart provides a guide to the recommended daily amounts of key nutrients. There are different nutritional requirements for infants, children under the age of four and pregnant and lactating women. Please talk to your doctor before changing your diet or the diet of your children.

* Recommended daily values can differ from country to country and from year to year; the information in the chart above is as recommended by the FDA. Please discuss any concerns with a health practitioner or your GP.

TOP 5 RECIPES FOR ESSENTIAL NUTRIENTS

Whole foods are a delicious source of natural energy, and they are packed full of nutrients to keep your body and mind functioning at their very best. Highlighted below are the top five recipes for seven key nutrients to support an active lifestyle.

TOP 5 RECIPES : POTASSIUM

A key electrolyte, potassium helps to regulate fluid levels in the body, manage blood pressure and is an important nutrient for heart health.

POTASSIUM RICH	DAILY VALUE IN ONE SERVING	PAGE NO.
Veg-Out Green Smoothie	26.00%	45
Get-Up-and-Green Juice	24.55%	52
Spice-it-Up Green Juice	34.02%	52
Rise-and-Shine Green Juice	29.26%	53
Drink Your Veggies	35.62%	55

TOP 5 RECIPES : DIETARY FIBRE

Only found in plant-based foods, fibre supports digestive health and helps to maintain a healthy weight.

EXCELLENT SOURCE OF DIETARY FIBRE	DAILY VALUE IN ONE SERVING	PAGE NO.
Red Velvet Smoothie	30%	36
Veg-Out Green Smoothie	33%	45
Coconut Raspberry Overnight Oats	57%	73
Perfect Pear Overnight Oats	42%	73
Decadent Chocolate Mousse	43%	153

TOP 5 RECIPES : PROTEIN

Proteins are the building blocks of our bodies and are essential for healthy growth and repair of our muscles, skin and internal organs.

PROTEIN RICH	DAILY VALUE IN ONE SERVING	PAGE NO.
Peanut Butter and Banana Porridge	19%	67
Banana Almond Crunch Overnight Oats	22%	71
Coconut Raspberry Overnight Oats	20%	73
Perfect Pear Overnight Oats	21%	73
Pepper and Garlic Chickpeas	18%	109

TOP 5 RECIPES : VITAMIN A

An essential, fat-soluble vitamin, vitamin A supports the immune system, vision and healthy growth.

EXCELLENT SOURCE OF VITAMIN A	DAILY VALUE IN ONE SERVING	PAGE NO.
Green Pumpkin Pie Smoothie	173%	37
Sweet Potato Power Smoothie	198%	37
Veg-Out Green Smoothie	167%	45
Carrot Ginger Soup	472%	48
Drink Your Veggies	187.22%	55

TOP 5 RECIPES : VITAMIN C

Vitamin C is an essential nutrient for the growth and repair of body tissue and also aids wound healing.

EXCELLENT SOURCE OF VITAMIN C	DAILY VALUE IN ONE SERVING	PAGE NO.
Peachy Green Smoothie	151%	33
Mango Refresher Slushy	164%	45
Veg-Out Green Smoothie	167%	45
Spice-it-Up Green Juice	216.27%	52
Rise-and-Shine Green Juice	139%	53

TOP 5 RECIPES : CALCIUM

The essential nutrient for bone health, calcium also helps our blood to clot and regulates muscle contraction.

CALCIUM RICH	DAILY VALUE IN ONE SERVING	PAGE NO.
Hot Chocolate with a Kick	48%	61
Chocolate Almond Butter Delight	50%	61
Peppermint Hot Chocolate	46%	63
Spiced Vanilla Almond Milk	51%	63
Healing Turmeric Latte	62%	63

TOP 5 RECIPES : IRON

The most important function of this essential mineral is its role in helping to make oxygen-carrying red blood cells.

IRON RICH	DAILY VALUE IN ONE SERVING	PAGE NO.
Green Apple Almond Smoothie	63%	32
Get-Up-and-Green Juice	43.25%	52
Spice-it-Up Green Juice	36.63%	52
Drink Your Veggies	87.75%	55
Healing Turmeric Latte	64%	63

INDEX OF RECIPES BY NUTRITIONAL TAG

Throughout the book, recipes are tagged for key nutritional qualities. The lists below are quick-reference guides for you to match a recipe with a particular goal, such as to sustain you through a long day or to give you an anti-inflammatory boost.

Slow-release Energy: Balanced to prevent blood sugar spikes and provide energy that lasts.

RECIPE	PAGE NO.
Smoothie Bowls	38
Chia Smoothies	43
Ice Cream Smoothies	49
Quinoa Breakfast Porridge	66
Grab-and-Go Overnight Oats	71
Baked Oat Cups	74
Out-and-About Muffins	76
Granolas	84
Trail Mixes	88
Supercharged Seed Mix	90
Hummus	95
Guacamole	99
Beetroot Dips	101
Cashew Cream Cheese	102
Breakfast Bars	114
Chewy Power Bars	117
Raw Fruit and Nut Bars	120
Make-Ahead Layered Parfaits	142
Decadent Chocolate Mousse	153
Chocolate Bark	154
DIY Nut Butter	160

Fast-release Energy: Recipes with a higher ratio of carbs to fat and protein.

RECIPE	PAGE NO.
Green Energy Smoothies	32
Slushy Smoothies	44
Green Juices	52
Red Juices	54
DIY Electrolyte Drinks	56
High-Energy Balls	126
Banana Ice Cream	146
Popsicles and Coconut Ice Cubes	150

Portable: Designed as grab-and-go options to be taken with you on a busy day.

RECIPE	PAGE NO.
Baked Oat Cups	74
Out-and-About Muffins	76
Granolas	84
Trail Mixes	88
Supercharged Seed Mix	90
Whole Food Crackers	92
Stuffed Dates	104
Roasted Chickpeas	108
Spiced Nuts	110
Breakfast Bars	114
Chewy Power Bars	117
Chocolate Energy Balls	124
Protein-Packed Cookies	140

Anti-inflammatory: The anti-inflammatory superstars – packed with omega-3s or healing spices.

RECIPE	PAGE NO.
Green Energy Smoothies	32
Berry-Licious Smoothies	34
Orange is the New Green	36
Smoothie Bowls	38
Chia Smoothies	43
Blended Soups	46
Green Juices	52
Healing Warming Drinks	60
Chia Seed Pudding	68
Grab-and-Go Overnight Oats	71
Whole Food Crackers	92
Hummus	95
Berry-Licious Chia Jam	106
Roasted Chickpeas	108
Spiced Nuts	110
Raw Fruit and Nut Bars	120
No-Nut Energy Bites	129
Chocolate Truffles	135

 Healthy Bones: Rich in calcium, magnesium and vitamins C and D, all essential for bone health.

RECIPE	PAGE NO.
Green Energy Smoothies	32
Berry-Licious Smoothie	34
Orange is the New Green	36
Smoothie Bowl	38
Ramp-it-Up Smoothies	41
Ice Cream Smoothies	49
Green Juices	52
Red Juices	54
Quinoa Breakfast Porridge	66
Chia Seed Pudding	68

 Muscle Repairing: A good source of protein for supporting muscle repair after exercise.

RECIPE	PAGE NO.
Chia Smoothies	43
Quinoa Breakfast Porridge	66
Frittata Cups	80
Hummus	95
Roasted Chickpeas	108

 Mood Enhancing: These recipes include whole foods that boost serotonin levels.

RECIPE	PAGE NO.
Ramp-it-Up Smoothies	41
Chia Smoothies	43
Blended Soups	46
Ice Cream Smoothies	49
Red Juices	54
Healing Warming Drinks	60
Chia Seed Pudding	68
Frittata Cups	80
Guacamole	99
Beetroot Dips	101
Chocolate Energy Balls	124
Chocolate Truffles	135
Frozen Banana Sandwiches	144
Banana Ice Cream	146
Healthy Chocolate Sauce	148
Decadent Chocolate Mousse	153
Chocolate Bark	154

GENERAL INDEX

fibre 36, 43, 71, 76, 78, 79,
   89, 90, 94, 106, 107,
   108, 116, 120, 128,129,
   133, 134, 147
   top 5 recipes 170
flavonoids 12, 135
flax egg 92
Frittata Cups
   Colourful Mixed Veggie
      80, **81**
   Go Green 82
   Southwestern 82
   Tomato Basil 80
Fruit
   dried 24, 117, 118
   frozen 24–25

G

Granola
   Almond Butter and
      Chocolate 87
   Buckwheat Crunchy 85
   Cashew Butter, Coconut,
      and Goji Berry 87
   Cranberry Orange
      Quinoa 86
   Sunflower Butter and Fig
      Spiced 87
   Three-Seed 86
   Vanilla Maple Crunch
      84, 85
Guacamole
   Classic 99
   Green on Green
      82, 100, **100**
   Salsa 99
   Tropical Treat 100

H

health food myth
   busting 16–19
Healthy Chocolate Sauce
   148, **149**
heart health 12, 25, 32, 35,
   102, 107, 111, 122
Hummus
   Garlicky **91**, 95
   Guacamole 95
   Roasted Red Pepper 96
   Spiced Roasted Carrot
      97, 98, **98**

Turmeric 96
hydration 43, 44, 45, 51, 55,
   56, 59, 151

I, J

immune system 52, 171
iron 119, 120
   top 5 recipes 171
Juice
   Anti-Inflammatory
      Green 52
   Drink Your Veggies 55
   Get-Up-and-Green **51**, 52
   Orange You Beet 55
   Refreshing Green 53, **53**
   Rice-and-Shine Green 53
   Spice-It-Up Green 52
   You Got the Beet **54**, 55

M

magnesium 9, 87, 129, 170,
   171, 173
manganese 107
monounsaturated fatty
   acids 122
Muffins
   Apple Spiced 79
   Chai Spiced Carrot 79
   Good Morning
      Blueberry 76
   Grain Free Gooey Banana
      Chocolate Chip 78
   Lemon Poppy Seed with
      Raspberries 77, **77**
   Millet 78

N

natural sweeteners 25
No-Nut Energy Bites
   Gingerbread Energy
      Bites 129, **130**
   Sesame Tahini Energy
      Bites **130**, 131
   Three-Seed Cherry
      Energy Bites 131
Nut Butter, DIY
   Basic Nut Butter 160
   Chocolate Hazelnut
      Butter 161

Cinnamon Cashew
   Butter 160
Salted Caramel
   Almond Butter 160
Sunflower Seed Butter 162
Vanilla Maple Walnut
   Butter 161
Nut Milk
   Basic Nut Milk 162
   Hazelnut and Chocolate
      Milk 164
   Hemp Seed Milk 164
   Spiced Brazil Nut
      Milk 164
   Strawberry Almond Milk
      163, 165
   Turmeric-Ginger Cashew
      Milk 165
   Vanilla Bean Cashew
      Milk 165
nutritional charts 168–173
nutritional information 8, 9
Nuts, Spiced
   Cacao-Dusted
      Almonds 112
   'Cheesy' Cashews 111
   Pizza on the Run 112
   Spicy Coconut Curry
      Cashews 110, **110**
   Spicy Mixed Nuts 111
   Sweet and Spicy Asian-
      Inspired Almonds 112
   Vanilla Orange
      Cashews 111

O

Oat Cups, Baked
   Apple Cinnamon 75
   Banana Chocolate Chip
      65, 74
   Lemony Blueberry 75
   Pumpkin Date 75
omega fatty acids 9, 43, 68,
   84, 106, 129, 131, 164
On-the-Go Super Seeds
   88, 90
Overnight Oats
   Banana Almond
      Crunch 71
   Blueberry Cashew 71, **72**
   Coconut Raspberry **72**, 73
   Perfect Pear 73

P

Parfait
   Blueberry Streusel
      142, 143
   Chocolate and Vanilla
      Pudding 143
   Spiced Fig Crunch 143
phytochemicals 12
phytonutrients 12, 32,
   55, 71
Popsicles
   Blueberry Coconut 152
   Grapefruit Mint 151
   Watermelon Burst
      150, 151
Porridge
   Apple, Cinnamon and
      Hazelnut Crumble
      66, **66**
   Berry, Coconut and
      Almond 67
   Peanut Butter and
      Banana 67
potassium 89, 128
   top 5 recipes 170
Power Bars
   Apricot and
      Sunflower 119
   Coconut, Almond and
      Chocolate 119
   Cranberry Pumpkin 119
   PB and J 117, **118**
probiotics 158
protein 9, 15, 18, 43, 66, 68,
   71, 78, 80, 90, 106,
   108, 109, 110, 123,
   126, 129, 131, 136,
   140, 155, 156, 162, 164
   top 5 recipes 170

R

Raw Fruit and Nut Bars
   Apricot, Vanilla and
      Cashew Bars 120, **121**
   Fudgy Brownie Bars 120
   Luscious Lemon Bars 121
   Spiced Cherry Pie
      Bars 121
   Strawberry Shortcake
      Bars 121

ACKNOWLEDGEMENTS

Along the way, some amazing people have provided support, dedication, enthusiasm and love to help me accomplish my dream of becoming a published author.

I'm grateful to Quantum Publishing for offering me this opportunity. A huge shout out to my editor, Philippa Davis. Thank you for guiding me through the entire process with your infinite wisdom and extreme patience.

Thank you to my parents, Beverly and Herbert Sturman, for encouraging me to follow my passion and start a second career even after footing the law school bills!

To my sea of guys – Steven, Noah and Daniel – who not only became my official recipe testers, but who also answered all my silly questions. There is a long list of reasons to thank you, but most importantly, thank you for believing in me and for being on this healthy journey together as a family. I love you.

To Heather White and Robynne Chutkan, two women who I am proud to call close friends, a big thanks for pushing me to say yes to this project.

To Rebecca Bailey, thank you for your strength with numbers and assistance with the nutritional data. Thank you Carina Muro for sharing your healthy baking secrets with me. To V Orban, a hug and thanks for all the laughs and fun we had in the kitchen.

To the *Kale & Chocolate* dream team, Gustavo 'Glass' Cejas and Jenny Carden, you've been by my side since day one!

To Monty and Cadence, my adorable Golden Retrievers, who kept me sane with each deadline and each day in between. Thank you for managing to keep the floors immaculate, even when the worktops were a complete mess.

Finally, thank you to my *Kale & Chocolate* Community. I never imagined that I would reach so many open-hearted and open-minded, incredible people to support and inspire me as I spread my message of health, happiness and love all over the world. This book is for you!

Quantum Books would like to thank the following for supplying images for inclusion in this book:

Shutterstock.com: Dudarev Mikhail 2-3, 29 below, 167; S_Photo 6-7; Maridav 13; denio109 22; Dionisvera 24 left; Alena Brozova 24 middle; Maya Kruchankova 24 right; Anna Shepulova 25; luminaimages 28; Alene Ozerova 29 above; matka_Wariatja 131; JPC-PROD 156; oliveromg 169 left; alexytrener 169 middle; Coffeemil 169 right; JeniFoto 171

Jackie Sobon 61

While every effort has been made to credit contributors, Quantum Books would like to apologize should there have been any omissions or errors and would be pleased to make the appropriate correction to future editions of the book.